TURNING POINTS

The
House
is
Quiet,
Now
What?

TURNING POINTS

JANICE HANNA
KATHLEEN Y'BARBO

The
House
is
Quiet,
Now
What?

REDISCOVERING LIFE AND ADVENTURE AS AN
EMPTY NESTER

BARBOUR
PUBLISHING

© 2009 by Barbour Publishing, Inc.

ISBN 978-1-60260-452-0

Published by Barbour Publishing, Inc., P.O. Box 719, Uhrichsville, Ohio 44683
www.barbourbooks.com

Our mission is to publish and distribute inspirational products offering exceptional value and biblical encouragement to the masses.

Member of the
Evangelical Christian
Publishers Association

Printed in the United States of America.

To my little birdies—Randi, Courtney Rae, Megan, and Courtney Elizabeth. You've given this mama bird wings to fly.
~Janice

May all who read these words find peace and a place of rest with the Lord, and may each of you look at this season of your life not as an emptying of the nest but as a place to wonder what the Lord will do next.
~Kathleen

Contents

OVERVIEW

The words of this book are bathed in prayer and were written with you in mind. They are divided into nine chapters, each specifically dealing with a particular subject empty-nest mothers face. Each chapter is divided into five sections:

- Bye-bye, Birdie: A section for the reader to take a look at the particular issue being addressed and acknowledge it for what it is in her life.

- Flight Patterns: A section filled with third-person stories of women just like you, who made it through the empty-nest season and came out victors on the other side.

- Spreading Your Wings: A section for the reader to erase any negative attitudes or feelings she's struggling with regarding that issue.

- Liftoff!: A section loaded with biblically based advice to help women overcome that particular issue.

- Smooth Sailing: Final words of encouragement to point the reader toward the One with the answers. Let the adventure begin!

We pray that you are able to read through this book with a happy heart, ready for a great adventure ahead. May your journey be all you dreamed. . .and more!

The greatest gifts you can give your children are
the roots of responsibility and the wings of independence.
DENIS WAITLEY

Introduction

*A child enters your home and for the next twenty years
makes so much noise you can hardly stand it. The child departs,
leaving the house so silent you think you are going mad.*
John Andrew Holmes

Ah, the empty-nest mom! She is the ultimate picture of
contradiction. For years she pushed, she prodded, she worked
around the clock to mold and shape her little darlings into real
people. . .people she could be proud of. Then, just about the time
she had them looking, acting, and smelling like adults. . .they flew
the coop!

Now she's free! Free to redecorate the nest, to nudge herself
over the edge, to do a little flying of her own. She's finally in a place
where she can rediscover her likes and dislikes, her dreams and
abilities. Best of all, she is in the perfect situation to fully develop
her relationship with the Lord.

Why, then, does she struggle?

Becoming an empty nester is tricky. It's an awesome, amazing,
freeing, terrible, horrible, no-good, very bad time. . .filled with
ups and downs, ins and outs. You're struggling to balance those
delicious feelings of freedom with the grief of watching your
children make their way into the world. . .without you! Talk about
a conundrum!

Think about the mama bird and her young. She works tirelessly
to nudge her babes from the nest, pushing them beyond their
limits. She's thrilled when they succeed. But the moment those
little darlings take to flight, she has second thoughts. "Wait a
minute!" she cries out. "Hold on! I wanted you to fly, but I didn't
mean for you to fly away!"

Poor mama bird. She sits in the nest, bemoaning the fact that her task—for the most part, anyway—is complete. She's worked herself out of a job. And now she is faced with the lingering question: What have I done? She mothered so well that she's left to suffer the consequences, whether she's psychologically prepared or not.

Chances are pretty good you can relate to that mama bird. As a mother, your world has been wrapped up in caring for the children God gave you. You sewed costumes for their ballet recitals, paid for guitar lessons, helped with homework, drove the carpool, spent countless hours at ballgames and other sporting events. You chose a van over a convertible and wore the team colors even when they clashed horribly with your complexion. In short, you gave up your very life for them.

And now they're gone. The ever-present sound of video games echoes in your mind, but the house is silent. There are no tennis shoes to trip over, no stinky laundry to toss into the washer, and no arguments to squelch. The sound of your daughter's voice chattering on the phone is only a distant memory, and you find yourself missing the hum of text messages coming through. Gone are the emergency poster-board runs on Sunday night, and the leftovers in the fridge are stacking up. You've washed that cheerleader outfit for the last time and packed your last school lunch. Your fall schedule includes Friday nights free, and there are no more pep rallies to attend. Worst of all, you're having to learn to cook for two again—or one, if you're single.

Yep. Watching those children fly away can be tough.

But it can also be freeing!

Suddenly you have your time back! You can set your own schedule, something that was impossible with a house full of kids. Those dreams you pressed to the back burner? You can pull them out again, dust them off, and look for the possibilities. You can travel! Take dance lessons! Join a bowling league. You can begin to focus once again on nurturing yourself—physically, spiritually, and emotionally. In short, you can take care of *you* for a change! And above all, you now have the time to pursue the most intimate relationship with the Lord you've ever known.

Yes, empty nester. . .tears will be shed. No doubt you will go through a bit of grieving, especially those of you who've been through a really traumatic experience (such as the death of a child or a sudden, unexpected tearing away). But don't let those tears fall because you think you're nothing without the children underfoot. Let it be because you miss them, plain and simple.

Mama Bird. . .it's time to fly!

Sweeter with Time
JANICE HANNA

Little one, little one, why must you grow?
So quickly it seems, the time must go,
But you grow sweeter with time.
Just let me hold you a little while longer,
To capture the moments God gives us each day.
And maybe someday, when I'm just a bit stronger,
I'll be prepared to watch you fly away.
Then you'll fly, little one, fly,
And be what God wants you to be.
He gave you to me to keep for a while,
To show us that His love will be
Sweeter. . .sweeter with time.

Chapter 1

YOU ARE NOT ALONE

It kills you to see them grow up.
But I guess it would kill you quicker if they didn't.
BARBARA KINGSOLVER

☾ BYE-BYE, BIRDIE!

As long as there have been mama birds and baby birds, there have been empty nests. Think about that for a moment. We can trace this empty-nest thing all the way back to the Garden of Eden, where the first mother had to learn to let go. (And talk about a traumatic story. One of her sons actually took the life of the other.)

You are in good company, Mom! Moses' mother had to say good-bye to her precious son—and at an early age, no less. Hannah surely agonized when she handed over young Samuel to Eli to raise. Ruth's mom had to release her daughter to the care of a mother-in-law. And Mary, the mother of Jesus, surely went through a difficult season where He left Nazareth to begin His ministry. Throughout time, women have carried, loved, and nurtured their children, then conquered the art of letting go. And who knows more about this empty-nest thing than the Lord Himself?

Consider the following story by Christian author Peggie C. Bohanon:

> *Once upon a time—and it's no fairy tale—a loving heavenly Father said to His Son, "Go! Leave this beautiful place called heaven. There's a lot of people down on earth who need Our love, Our help—and Our redemptive plan. Go—save the world; bring them back to Me. I've got a wonderful plan, but You must leave home for it to work!"*
>
> *And leave He did. Our Savior left the ivory palaces to come to our dirty, grungy world. . .right where we live. He*

left the nest—but it was necessary, for God had a plan, a plan with purpose, to one day fill that nest again—with folk like you and me! Thank God He emptied heaven's nest so we could be included—and thank God that He knows how it feels! Remember, whether you're a mom, dad, grandma, grandpa emptying the nest—or you're the kid leaving the nest—He knows![1]

Doesn't that just thrill your soul? The God of heaven knows exactly how you feel. He's walked a mile in your shoes, figuratively speaking. Only, in His case, He knew that His Son would die for the sins of the world. Still, His Father's heart surely ached as Jesus stepped out of heaven onto earth's shore.

So you see, Mama Bird. . .you are certainly not alone!

Consider Gillian's story: Gillian was every kid's dream mom. When her son and daughter were elementary-school age, she opened her home—and her heart—to their friends, becoming known as "the Kool-Aid mom." She was president of the PTA, taught their Sunday school class, sang goofy songs in the car, and kept her kids entertained for hours on road trips. She kissed away their boo-boos, dried their tears, and tucked them into bed at night. And then there were the junior-high years! She took her daughter shopping for her first bra, walked her son through his first crush on a girl, and paid for piano lessons, guitar lessons, and more.

In short, she poured out her life for them.

---

[1] "The God of the Empty Nest!" by Peggie C. Bohanon, *http://www.peggiesplace.com/booster116.htm.*

18

When they morphed into teens, Gillian walked alongside them every step of the way. She taught them to drive, helped them paint their bedrooms crazy colors, put up with their mood shifts, and even chaperoned youth group ski trips. She watched a host of potential boyfriends and girlfriends come and go, and even helped her daughter select a prom dress when the time came. By the time her youngest graduated from high school, Gillian was tired. . .but thrilled. With the help of her husband (and the Lord, of course), she'd raised two beautiful adults. Time to push them out of the nest.

Unfortunately, no one told Gillian that she should begin preparing for the empty nest while her son and daughter were still at home. So, when her daughter left for college, Gillian had a meltdown. Little things—like watching other moms sitting next to their teens in church—nearly proved to be her undoing. And big things, family functions without her son or daughter in attendance, were much tougher than she'd imagined.

She missed her son most keenly during basketball season. And her daughter? Going to the mall without her was just plain boring. Gillian particularly missed their late-night chats and impromptu talks about boyfriends. Sure, she was thrilled at this new opportunity—to renew her relationship with her husband and explore new plans for her own life. But in the secret, quiet moments, she still longed for the pitter-patter of little feet around the house. She wouldn't even mind tripping over her son's size 12 basketball shoes.

Maybe your situation is different from Gillian's. Perhaps you're thrilled to finally have your house to yourself. You can hardly wait to take possession of their bedrooms, converting them into an office or media room. You've already set plans in motion for a trip to Europe or a cruise to the Caribbean.

Or maybe it's just the opposite. Perhaps your case is even more extreme than Gillian's. You find yourself overly weepy, agonizing as you look at the stuffed bunny on your daughter's bed. . .the one she decided she could do without in her college dorm.

Regardless, the empty-nest years are filled with change, and change is never easy.

The Bible is clear that children are only ours for a season. They live with us, learn from us, and tend to act like us. (Scary, isn't it!) And we're blessed to have them for that period of time. Though many moms wish their mothering could go on a bit longer, there comes that inevitable moment when we must cut the strings.

But when? At what age? How long does the child-rearing season last? That varies from family to family, child to child. After all, not all kids are the same. Some are ready to face the world at eighteen; some aren't ready till they're twenty-eight! Without our insistence, there are probably some who would postpone their flight from the nest indefinitely. We have to walk them through the transition from childhood to adulthood, then determine—together—when the time is right to let go.

So, what is your situation, Mom? Has your son or daughter left for college? Are you one of those whose teenager opted to live elsewhere? Maybe you've been in a great relationship with your child, but now he or she is married. Or maybe you've just reached the point where it was time to tell that twenty-something he had to find a new place to live. ASAP.

Regardless, the transition from full house to empty nest is an interesting and tumultuous one. In many ways, it's like a roller coaster ride, filled with some high highs and some low lows. The highs can be exhilarating, but plummeting down into depression is not.

Maybe you're thrilled with the idea of having your time— and your home—to yourself. Or maybe you're struggling, wondering how you will find yourself without kids in the picture. If you're one of those moms whose entire identity is tied up with your children, this process will likely be very emotional. If you're one of those moms who has had it with parenting and is ready for some downtime, congratulations! You're about to get the chance of a lifetime!

When mothers talk about the depression of the empty nest, they're not mourning the passing of all those wet towels on the floor, or the music that numbs your teeth, or even the bottle of capless shampoo dribbling down the shower drain. They're upset because they've gone from supervisor of a child's life to a spectator. It's like being the vice president of the United States.

ERMA BOMBECK

◯ SPREADING YOUR WINGS

When you think about your journey into the empty-nest years, what comes to mind? Excitement? Fear? Confusion?

Without the kids in the house, do you feel alone? Wish you could have them back? Or are you thrilled for the additional time and space? If you're struggling with feelings of aloneness, it's good to look at when and where, so that you know how best to cope. Take a look at the following list of things that empty nesters struggle with:

- The first day (or week or year) after your child leaves for college

- The first day (or week or year) after your child marries

- Your child's empty bedroom

- Family functions without your child in attendance

- Trips to the mall—alone

- Friends who still have kids at home

- The onset of a particular sports season

- Bedtime

- Mealtime

- Having the remote control all to yourself

- No one to laugh with

- Things out of reach (It's nice to have given birth to people taller than you.)

- Early mornings, when the house is quiet

There are certainly times when you're going to miss those kiddos. But remember. . .life moves in seasons. And the Lord promises to walk with you through every one.

◐ LIFTOFF!

Let's go back and look at that list of times and places where empty-nest moms struggle. We're going to put those things in perspective and give some solutions.

- *The first day (or week or year) after your child leaves for college.* When your child leaves for college, you will go through some inevitable shifts—both in your thinking and in your living arrangements. Instead of focusing on your empty house, get busy! Your son or daughter is in school. Learning. Growing. Is it time for you to do the same? Is there a course you've been longing to take at your local community college? An art class? A creative writing course? Now is the time. And even if you don't feel led to further your own education, use this time to help your son or daughter through this pivotal year. Set up a plan of action to send gift baskets with things from home. Bake cookies. Buy socks or fun things to lift the spirits. Make this an "educational" time for the whole family.

- *The first day (or week or year) after your child marries.*
  When your child marries, you're bound to feel a little
  lost. Why not use the word *marriage* as a trigger to build
  up your own marriage (if you have a spouse, of course).
  This is the perfect opportunity. Consider yourselves as
  honeymooners. (And you are, to some extent! You've
  got the house back to yourselves!) Begin to think like a
  honeymooner. Plan a vacation together or make your
  bedroom a romantic hideaway. And if you're not married,
  think about the fact that you are the bride of Christ. Work
  on *that* relationship. He longs to sweep you away into His
  courts, to call you His beloved, His bride.

- *Your child's empty bedroom.* There are so many memories
  attached to things like stuffed animals, trinkets, and even
  wall colors and bedding. And this can be a tricky issue.
  If your child is going to be coming and going from the
  house, you might not want to strip down the room right
  away. On the other hand, maybe you've been waiting for
  the perfect opportunity to create a home office or a sewing
  room. Can you replace the double bed with a twin and
  accommodate both needs? That way your son or daughter
  will still have a place to sleep, but you can create your
  dream room, too.

- *Family functions without your child in attendance.* These
  events might be tough, but they present the perfect
  opportunity to develop stronger relationships with the
  other people in your family. With each outing, choose

one person from the family to spend extra/quality time with. Focus on that person's life, needs, joys, and sorrows. Really connect with him or her. You'll be surprised at how little time you spend missing your kids when you're truly connecting with others. If they're still alive, this is the perfect opportunity to rediscover your parents. They have so much wisdom to share!

- *Trips to the mall—alone.* They can be a lot of fun! Yes, really! Likely, you've spent the last few years shopping in stores you weren't crazy about (to appease the kids). Now you can pick where you go, how long you stay there, and which departments to frequent. And there's nothing better than shopping with a good friend. Take a look at Tasha's story:

  My daughter and I loved to hang out at our local Super Center and at the mall. The first time I had to go shopping after she left for college, I found myself actually getting teary-eyed! (Sounds goofy, I know.) Anyway, I made up my mind I would make shopping a pleasurable experience. The next time I went to the mall, I deliberately went into stores that I'd avoided when we were together (stores I knew she didn't care to shop in, I mean). I found myself discovering a whole new world!

- *Friends who still have kids at home.* Hanging out with these friends can be a challenge, especially if their kids are in and out of the house a lot. You're in a different season,

25

but that's not a bad thing. It's part of the experience. Instead of feeling sorry for yourself, begin to enjoy—really enjoy—your friends' kids. You'll be surprised at how those relationships can grow.

- *The onset of a particular sports season.* Is basketball season tough on you? Baseball? Hockey? Moms who've raised sports-minded kids can really struggle during such seasons. Maybe you're facing the fact that for the first time you won't be needing those season tickets to the high-school football game. Go anyway. True, you won't be cheering for your child running on the field or playing an instrument at halftime. But you can still have a great time.

- *Bedtime.* When the nest empties, bedtime can be lonely, but it doesn't have to be. This is a great time for bubble baths, great books, and romantic encounters (if you're married, of course). Isn't it wonderful not to have to rush to the store for last-minute school things? And aren't you glad the washer isn't running late into the night? Nighttimes for the empty nester can be peaceful and soothing. Ah, what luxury! Take a look at this story from an empty nester named Charlotte:

  As a single mom, I'd always enjoyed the evenings. Making sure the kids were tucked in. Kissing them goodnight. Then came that inevitable day when the little birdies weren't there anymore. I knew they were safe and sound in their own beds—one just a few miles away and

*the other in another state—but I still paced the house
at night, praying for them and worrying. God finally
released me from that. I'll be honest. . .it took time. But
He convinced me that He was their covering, not me. I
had to let go and trust Him. . .completely trust Him!*

- *Mealtime.* Do you struggle during meals? Maybe you're
  accustomed to cooking for a large crowd but need to scale
  down. Here's one way to remedy that. Go ahead and cook
  your meals, as always. Take half of what you've cooked and
  freeze it. That way you've prepared two meals for the price
  of one. At least once a week, use the fine china. Turn the
  lights down and use romantic candles. (Hey, this works,
  even if you're not married. Why not enjoy the ambience
  of a good meal by candlelight?) Turn on some soothing
  music. And if you're really struggling with having fewer
  people at the table, why not set a certain night of the week
  to meet a friend for dinner or to invite an elderly neighbor
  over for pot roast and potatoes? You'll have a home-cooked
  meal and great dinner conversation! Here's one more
  suggestion: if you really love to cook, why not volunteer
  at a local homeless shelter? The people there would be
  thrilled to have you. Those "big" meals you've always loved
  putting together? Imagine serving them to a roomful of
  hungry folks who haven't eaten for days! Talk about being
  appreciated!

- *Having the remote control all to yourself.* Oh, what a joy, to
  finally be able to choose what shows you want to watch

. . .and when. Haven't watched television in years? The choices are practically unlimited these days. Peruse the television guides and choose a few to "visit" until you find the ones you like. Don't like what's on television? Make at least one night per week movie night! Or, better yet, read a good book. You'll soon find which type of evening entertainment suits you. And, as with most of the suggestions for activities in this book, half the fun is in the discovery.

- *No one to laugh with.* When there's no one to laugh with, laugh anyway. Your pet will think you've lost your mind, but even that's something to smile at. No pet? Laugh anyway. No one's looking, so really let go. Start with a giggle if you're feeling intimidated by the prospect, and in time you'll be laughing out loud without caring who is—or isn't—around. Go ahead. Make a joyful noise! (This is especially fun if you're reading silly e-mails or watching a comedy on television!)

- *Things out of reach.* Can't reach something? Get a step stool. If that's not an option, then find lower places to store things. Or, even better, toss things that are stored down low and put what remains within your reach. The adjustments will be well worth the results.

- *Early mornings, when the house is quiet.* You may be tempted to think of what it used to be like when breakfast was more of a race than a sole endeavor. No longer is a lineup of bacon, eggs, and backpacks filling the kitchen.

Those first moments of the day can now be filled with other things, like connecting with the Creator. Use the time you might have been packing lunches to open the Bible and immerse yourself in the Word. Take a look at Louise's story:

Mornings used to be pretty chaotic. Five kids. A waiting school bus. School lunches. Mismatched socks. Missing shoes. Missing homework papers. You name it, we faced it. . .for years! Now that the kids are gone, the mornings are strangely quiet. It took me the longest time to realize that was a gift, not a curse! I now have the time to truly connect with God before I start my day—with no interruptions!

See? God has a way of taking your "aloneness" and using it for His glory. So take heart! Your nest might have emptied, Mama Bird, but that doesn't mean you've lost your hatchlings. Yes, there will be adjustments, and many will not be easy. Make this season an adventure. Find new ways to appreciate this time of your life, and soon you will be wondering what all the chirping was about.

◖ FLIGHT PATTERNS

> *Graduation day is tough for adults. They go to the*
> *ceremony as parents. They come home as contemporaries.*
> *After twenty-two years of child-rearing, they are unemployed.*
> ERMA BOMBECK

So, your little birdies have flown the coop and your nest is feeling pretty empty. You're torn about the role you now play—or don't play—in the life of your child or children. Maybe this is a good time to analyze your ever-changing role. One way you can do this is by studying the various ways others have made the jump.

Different people have different methods of coping. For the sake of this book, we're going to call those methods "Flight Patterns." Maybe your pattern will include starting a new career or redecorating the house. Some moms might start a hobby or join a Bible study. Regardless, it's fun to look at how others have met the challenges of the empty nest so that you can see you're not alone. Perhaps you will learn from their experiences. Or their mistakes.

Consider these words from an empty nester by the name of Bonnie:

> *A mother who "hovers" is a mother who is teaching*
> *her child to be dependent in a way that isn't good for the*
> *child. Our goal as mothers should be to teach our children*
> *a "can-do" attitude that will send them into the world*
> *feeling capable and dependent on the Lord. . .not on*
> *Mommy. When to stop mothering? When the children can*
> *do it themselves.*

Stopping mothering should begin when a child is very small if we are talking about the "doing for." If we are talking about the "praying for" and the offering emotional support part of mothering, I don't think that ever ends. My grown children know that I am here for them. I will listen and pray and support in any way I can, but they are adults now and responsible for their own lives, and mothering does not include guilt trips put on them if they don't call or write or visit often enough to please me. It does not include "dump your laundry here on your way through between the dorm and the mall."

Mothering means teaching children to gradually accept responsibility for themselves. It means holding them in our hearts forever. . .but never holding them back, never creating dependence. Mothering means teaching them to fly and refusing to make them feel guilty for leaving the nest.

Isn't that an interesting perspective? And doesn't it help you take a step back, allowing your child to take the reins?

Another empty-nest mom gave this advice to deal with feelings of aloneness:

Out with the old and in with the new. I'm a firm believer in doing things. . .and doing them quickly. When my daughter left for college, she packed her things away in the attic, pointed at her empty room, and said, "Have at it, Mom." And have at it, I did! I quickly converted the space into a long-awaited quilting room. (I'd been quilting for years but never had adequate space.) I knew that keeping the room filled with my daughter's things would've been psychologically taxing, anyway. I could just see myself going in there every morning, picking up her stuffed animals and blubbering all over them. So, this was a better option for me. (Out of sight, out of mind, right?)

Our daughter still comes home from college on holidays, of course. The first time she saw her converted room, it threw her a little bit. And sleeping on the sofa bed isn't really her cup of tea. But overall, she's taken the transition pretty well. So have I, actually.

Can you see how both of these women handled the transition into the empty-nest years? Let's take a look at one more woman's reaction to this life-shift. Here is Cathy's story:

I always loved being a mommy, and I still do! My daughter calls every day and we relate as both parent/ child and friends. I can devote my "mommy-ing" to my two grandchildren and I regularly "adopt" other kids from school. I've just retired as a teacher, and every year the Lord sent me someone to minister to.

And as I think of it, that was the major way God got me through the absence of my biological child. For several years I'd have some student who really attached him- or herself to me, and I shared Christ and his or her triumphs and sorrows.

Different strokes for different folks! No doubt about that! How you react to this season is as individual as your personality. In other words, there is no "right" or "wrong" way to do this. No formula. Just be yourself, Mom. God will get you through this. In fact, He will meet you right where you are.

◯ SMOOTH SAILING

So, what do you think, Mom? Think you're going to make it through this season of your life? With God's help, you will! He wants you to know that He's right here with you. Though your house might seem big—empty, even—you're not alone.

Take a look at the following scriptures. Write them on slips of paper and tape them to your refrigerator, your bathroom mirror, or any other place where you might see them on a regular basis. Memorize them so they're handy when you need them. May they be a constant reminder that your work as a mom has been—and will continue to be—a blessing.

- *And when he had sent the multitudes away, he went up into a mountain apart to pray: and when the evening was come, he was there alone.*
  MATTHEW 14:23 KJV

- *God has said, "Never will I leave you; never will I forsake you." So we say with confidence, "The Lord is my helper; I will not be afraid. What can man do to me?"*
  HEBREWS 13:5–6 NIV

- *A time to weep and a time to laugh, a time to mourn and a time to dance.*
  ECCLESIASTES 3:4 NIV

> *The best way to keep children at home is to make the home atmosphere pleasant, and let the air out of the tires.*
> DOROTHY PARKER

Chapter 2

Redefining and Rediscovering

*Soon after our last child left home for college, my husband
was resting next to me on the couch with his head in my lap.
I carefully removed his glasses. "You know, Honey," I said sweetly,
"without your glasses, you look like the same handsome young
man I married." "Honey," he replied with a grin, "without
my glasses, you still look pretty good, too!"*
UNKNOWN

◖ BYE-BYE, BIRDIE

Oh, that empty-nest season! It's the perfect time to redefine—your life, your relationship with God, your marriage, your friendships, and even your home. It's also a great time to rediscover—your calling, your gifts, your passions and hobbies. What a glorious opportunity for new and exciting things! Seeing them as new and exciting, however, might take a little work.

Going through major life-shifts, especially at this age, can be a bit daunting. After all, you've only recently discovered that your whole world is not just about you and your children. But you can make it. You just need to redefine your role as a woman. And it's time for a major shift in attitude. Your kids are grown . . .and that's okay! No point in fretting about it. (And by the way, you're much more likely to fret if you don't take the time to redefine your attitude.) Don't set your sights on the past. Look to the future. But when you do, don't look at it with the words, *I see the future and I don't like it*, in mind. Instead, look at it as filled with possibilities.

It's true that your family unit—as you knew it—is changing before your eyes, but that's a good thing. And yes, you will grieve a little as each child moves away. Part of that grieving involves the revelation that you're aging. You find yourself saying things like, "Oh my goodness, I'm old enough to have a kid who (fill in the blank)." First it's "go to kindergarten," then "date," "get a driver's license," "get that first job." From there, it shifts to things like "go to college," "get married," "have a baby," etc. Time to redefine aging, perhaps?

They're growing up, Mom. And so are you! And there is

no better time than now to rediscover who you really are. To redefine your purpose and your role.

To *redefine* means "to give a new or different definition to."[22] When you redefine something, you have to carefully rethink it so that you can give it the best definition possible. Now think about the word *rediscover*. When you *re*discover something, you're discovering it all over again. It's almost like you had a wonderful treasure, tucked it away for a while, then suddenly discovered it was there all over again. That's exactly what this season is. A rediscovery.

So, what dreams did you push to the background so that you could focus on your kids? When you think back to your childhood or teen years, what did you always say you wanted to be—or do—when you grew up? (Short of being a mother, of course.) Now is the time to reawaken that dream!

This is an amazing opportunity to begin again, to peer out over the edge of the nest you've been safe and comfortable in. And you're certainly not the only mother to get this amazing chance. In fact, the Bible is filled with stories of women who decided to shift into a new gear. Think about Naomi, Ruth's mother. She went through a terrible tragedy when she lost her sons. But her relationship with Ruth, her daughter-in-law, was just what she needed to get her through the pain. Overcoming that sense of loss came as she rediscovered herself. . .as a mother-in-law and eventually as a proud grandmother.

Remember Gillian? She had a hard time letting go when her kids went off to college. And when the youngest got married, she

<hr>

[2] *The Free Online Dictionary*, s.v. "redefine," *www.thefreedictionary.com/redefine* (accessed April 20, 2009).

really had a meltdown. In the months that followed, she tried to fill the void with a variety of different things—food, friends, television, books. Nothing worked. Gillian's relationship with the Lord waned for a while, but after some time, she began to seek Him regarding her current situation.

The Lord, of course, responded (just as He always does when we seek Him). He lifted Gillian out of the pit and, through the comfort of the Holy Spirit, gave her the wherewithal to begin redefining her life. Before long, she joined a women's Bible study at church. A year and a half later, she was teaching the Bible study. On top of this, she began to redefine herself in other ways. Gillian hadn't finished college, but this season gave her the perfect opportunity. With fear and trembling, she entered the college scene once again. It scared her to death at first, but she eventually got in the groove and began to enjoy it. In fact, she was teacher's pet. . .one with a lot of new friends.

Then came the biggest change of all. Gillian began to redefine her relationship with her husband. Though his work schedule didn't give him as much free time, they took advantage of the time they did have together. Before long, they began to take trips, go to conferences, and even went on a second honeymoon to Grand Cayman. Talk about a blast!

Like so many others who've already walked this road before you, it's time! Time to spread your wings and fly. The very thing you've been training your kids to do is now *yours* to do! C'mon, Mom! Let's go!

◯ SPREADING YOUR WINGS

There are no birds in last year's nest.
HENRY WADSWORTH LONGFELLOW

Take a look at the quote above by Henry Wadsworth
Longfellow. Might sound strange, but it's true. There are no
birds in last year's nest. Life moves forward. . .and in seasons at
that. You've probably heard this scripture from Ecclesiastes 3:1
all of your life: "There is an appointed time for everything. And
there is a time for every event under heaven" (NASB). It's so true!
And you happen to be in a new and glorious season. Your nest is
empty, but your heart can be very, very full.

Mom, this season calls for redefining and rediscovering.
Perhaps you hear those words and feel a little clueless. You'd like
to have a second chance—with relationships, talents, and so
forth—but don't know where to begin. There's really only one
way to go about this. You have to break down the individual
areas of your life and examine each one. Each is an opportunity
for rediscovery. And some might take more work than others!

So, where will you begin? With your spiritual life? Your
relationships? Your hobbies? The possibilities are endless. Why
not take a look at the following list of areas you might consider
and then decide:

- Your relationship with God (Can you see it deepening
  over time?)

- Your self/your purpose (After all, we often don't know who we are at this stage.)

- Your marriage (Let the sparks fly!)
- Your time (You're liable to have more of it, and that's a good thing!)
- Your career (Hmm. I wonder what I want to be when I grow up?)
- Your spiritual gifts (You have some, you know!)
- Your house (home remodeling)
- Your health (joining a gym and/or dieting)
- Your place in the body of Christ (missions, etc.)
- Your relationships with parents, siblings, and other family members
- Your friendships (with both new friends and old)
- Learning a new skill (computers, photography, dance lessons, etc.)
- Hobbies (Yes! You finally have the time!)
- Volunteering (The possibilities are endless.)

Whew! There's a lot to think about, isn't there? So, what do you think, Mom? Do any of these sound intriguing? Can you see yourself spreading your wings and taking flight in a few of these areas? If so, then hang on! You're about to soar!

◖ LIFTOFF!

So, what's on your list? What have you secretly (or not so secretly) longed to do? Teach a Bible study? Travel? Spend more time in prayer? Learn to play the piano? Sing in a choir? Deepen your relationship with God? Decorate cakes? Take line-dancing lessons? Research your family's lineage? Take a pottery class? Join a photography group? Join the YMCA? Run for a neighborhood committee? It's time to figure out what you used to like to do and who you always said you wanted to be when you grew up.

When you rediscover yourself (something that only happens through prayer), you find that there are plenty of things you have yet to try.

Let's take another look at this list, this time looking at a few suggestions to help you redefine those areas.

- *Your relationship with God.* These years aren't just about rediscovering your gifts. They're about getting reignited in your relationship with God. Even if you're working full-time, it's likely you'll now have more time to truly focus on your quiet time and Bible reading. Maybe you could sign up for an online Bible class, or at the very least, an online devotional. Perhaps you could start something like that, instead! Maybe you've always wanted to join the women's ministry at your church but didn't have time. Surely those women had walked with you through your child-rearing years. Another great way to strengthen your spiritual growth is to memorize scriptures. One of the biggest hurdles, of course, is to get over being mad at the Lord, if you are. Take your angst to Him. Perhaps you feel you didn't do the best job raising your kids and long for a second chance. Give your regrets to the Lord. Perhaps you're thrilled with the way your kids turned out, but secretly long for more time with them. Express those desires to the Lord. Approach your heavenly Father with both your thanksgiving and your regret. Let them go at His altar. Then watch as your relationship with God is deepened. As you think about these things, take a look at Melinda's story:

Our family was in church every time the doors were open. My kids came to know the Lord at an early age, something I've always been thankful for. It wasn't until my youngest moved off to another state that I realized something. For some time—I'm not sure how long—I'd been going to church out of rote. Don't get me wrong. I loved the Lord and didn't realize that's what I was doing. . .but it was. I asked the Lord to forgive me and decided to stop going through the motions. I truly started worshipping. Truly started reaching out to others in love. Truly listened to the messages. . .with my whole heart. In a sense, I came alive again.

- *Your self/your purpose.* The empty-nest years provide the perfect opportunity to think about your purpose in life. It's time for a renewal! Think about the calling God has placed on your life. What were you created to do (short of being a mom, that is)? Your calling defines your purpose.

A lot of empty-nest moms have lost their sense of purpose. They can't seem to remember why they were put on planet Earth. You were created to worship God and to reflect His love to the world. Redefining your relationship with Him will help you rediscover your purpose. Sometimes we're so busy that we stop thinking about our calling. Consider Marti's story:

I'll be honest. . . . I was depressed when my kids left home. I'd spent twenty-five years mothering and wasn't sure what to do with myself when they were gone. Sure, I had my job, and it was a nice distraction, but as a single woman, I couldn't really figure out where I fit in. So, I spent my free time at home alone, watching reality television and hiding under the covers. My doctor—who was worried about my health—finally put me on medication for depression. It helped a little. Then, the most amazing thing happened! A friend from church invited me to a Sunday school class that focused on missions. They were planning a trip to Kenya and asked if I wanted to go along. I agreed to pray about it, which I did with fear and trembling. I came up with a thousand excuses why this would never work, but in the end, I bought my plane ticket and went to Kenya with the group—kicking and screaming, I might add. What happened next changed my life forever. It might not sound grandiose, but it was to me. I handed out toothbrushes to children. Toothbrushes! And I taught the children how to brush their teeth. (My mothering skills came in handy

once again!) Seeing those kids—and realizing that I could
make a difference in their lives—changed my attitude. It
lit a flame underneath me and helped me put things in
perspective. When we got home to Texas, I could hardly
wait for the next trip. I've since taken eleven trips to
Africa and plan to go back this summer. Oh, and my
depression medication? I tossed it. No need for it anymore!
Shifting my focus led to rediscovering my purpose. I've
never looked back since. (And isn't it funny how God
could use a toothbrush to change a person's life?)

The truth is, God can use anything He chooses to change
our lives, right? And He does. . .if we let Him.

- *Your marriage.* This is a great time to rediscover your
  mate. Even if it's been awhile since you've been intimate
  (and some couples with high schoolers have reached the
  point where their love life has taken a backseat), there's
  now time for that second-honeymoon phase. No longer
  are you focused on your children's activities, their school
  functions, and/or their friends. Now you can focus on
  nurturing your relationship with your husband. Plan
  a weekend away at a bed and breakfast. Start a mutual
  hobby. Find something you used to want to do together
  and do it, even if you don't think you will like it. Go on
  dates. Get intimate. Recall that first year. Only, you know
  more now. Your relationship can be the best it has ever
  been! Consider this story from a woman named Kate:

> *I enjoyed my time with our children at home. My
> life revolved around their activities, their lives, their
> school, their friends. One thing I tried not to lose sight
> of was that there would come a day when it would just
> be my husband and me again. Together we nurtured
> that relationship as much as possible: date nights, some
> time away as a couple when Grandma could babysit,
> listening and caring for the other's joys and sorrows. Now
> that we are empty nesters, we are reaping the rewards.
> Our relationship is deeper and closer than ever after forty
> years and fills the spots left vacant by our grown children
> leaving home.*

- *Your time.* Ready to redefine and rediscover your time?
  You've got more of it now, if you're like most empty
  nesters—time to volunteer, to devote to your husband,
  your work, and your church. Many empty nesters spend
  their free time traveling, prompting their children to ask
  things like, "Where are Mom and Dad?" And so be it!
  Follow your travel dreams! Where did you always want
  to go? On an RV trip around the country? Fly to Italy?
  Maybe you couldn't afford to do these things with a
  houseful of kids. Now's the time to start deciding whether
  some dreams were just good ideas or real possibilities
  (although a few of them might not be as appealing to you
  now). Of course, not everyone is ready to hit the road
  when that last child goes off to college or gets married.
  Maybe your travel plans include saving toward an RV or
  a place at the lake. Begin to create goals! Soon enough,

those dreams will become realities. Maybe this is the time to start taking weekend trips. Perhaps you can turn visits with your children into fun and exciting travel opportunities. Regardless. . .hit the road, Jack. And don't look back! There's plenty of adventure ahead.

- *Your career.* The empty-nest years give you the perfect opportunity to develop and/or grow in your career. Pam Farrel, founder of Seasonedsisters.com, an organization to encourage women in life's second half, has this to say in her book *Fantastic After 40!*:

> *Madame Curie created the scientific study of radioactivity, and she was the first woman to be given the Nobel Peace Prize. She is the first, and only, woman to win it twice—the second time at the age of 44. Condoleezza Rice took the office of National Security Advisor to the president when she was 47. Jenny Craig began her multimillion-dollar weight loss business after her fortieth birthday, and now millions of women over 40 are grateful. . . . You can't even be president of the United States until you are 35, and the vast majority of our presidents took office well after their fortieth year of life. (Who's going to run for office, girls?)* [3]

Don't you love that? The middle years are the perfect time to "grow" your career. Think of the many women you know who have thrived in the business world. And you can be among

[3] Pam Farrel, *Fantastic After 40!: The Savvy Woman's Guide to Her Best Season of Life* (Eugene, Oregon: Harvest House Publishers, 2007), 12. Used with permission.

them. . .if this is your desire and the Lord's plan for you. Trust Him in this. He will lead the way.

- *Your spiritual gifts.* It's likely you've been operating your spiritual gifts for years and haven't even realized it. You've always had a teacher's heart, of course. That's what being a mom is all about. But it's likely you're also an encourager or have an abundance of wisdom and discernment. This is the perfect opportunity to do a thorough study of the spiritual gifts. Start by reading Romans 12, 1 Corinthians 12, and Ephesians 4. Then ask the Lord to show you which of those gifts comes most naturally to you. There are a host of online tests that can help you rediscover your spiritual gifts. This is also a great time to ask friends and family members for their input. Likely, they know your gifts. . .even if you don't!

- *Your house.* Time to redefine your living space? Some empty nesters trade in their three-, four-, or five-bedroom homes for something smaller. (After all, they don't need all of those rooms, and living in a particular school district is no longer an issue.) Those who stay put often redefine the space they already have. Many empty nesters see this season as the perfect opportunity—to tear down walls, restructure bedrooms into offices or media rooms, to build a deck in the backyard. Take a look at Nicole's story:

> *My mother always wanted a sewing room. I heard about it all of my life. Imagine my surprise when I came*

*back from college one semester to find she'd converted
my old room into her new space! Sure, she'd left a twin
bed for me, but the rest of the room was completely
transformed. It took me awhile to adjust to this new
idea, but it was her house, after all. Now, years later,
I can see so clearly how God has used that space for my
mom's growth. She's crafted all sorts of great things in her
sewing room, and I wouldn't take that away from her for
anything!*

- *Your health.* Many empty-nest moms find this the perfect
season to get in shape and/or take better care of themselves
physically. Perhaps join a gym. Maybe even hire a personal
trainer. It's a great time to reexamine that body of yours, to
see what fine-tuning or honing could take place. Sure, there
are some things you can't control, but diet, exercise, and
a great attitude? These are all great for your health. Why
not visit with your doctor soon to ask for his or her advice?
Then, get moving!

- *Your place in the body of Christ.* A lot of empty-nest women
feel lost at church (often because they've always been
known as "Johnny's mom" or "Susie's mom"). It's time to
reidentify yourself! Take a look at the various ministries
of your church. Where is your best fit? Perhaps you've
always wanted to work in children's church but didn't have
the energy with a houseful of your own kids. Maybe you
have a winning smile and could work as a greeter. Perhaps
you've put off going to the mission field because you didn't

have the time or the money. Examine all of these options. . .
and more! Take a look at Joanna's story:

> *Might sound funny, but I never worked in children's
> ministry when my kids were little. I always felt a little
> guilty about that, but as a homeschool mother of four, my
> church time was truly my only time away from the kids.
> Now that they're grown, something funny has happened.
> I was asked to take over the children's church program.
> I had to laugh, in part because God has such a sense of
> humor and in part because I actually want to do it!*

- *Your relationships with parents, siblings, and other family
  members.* How long has it been since you sat down and
  worked on your family tree? There's nothing like it to
  stir your feelings for family members. And when was the
  last time you picked up the phone and called a brother, a
  sister, a parent, or a cousin? The empty-nest years are the
  perfect time to get reacquainted with those long-distance
  relatives you haven't seen in years. To call your sister
  more frequently. To take your mom to lunch. Even if you
  haven't had a good relationship with family members, God
  can use this special season to redefine those connections.
  Ask for His input today.

- *Your friendships.* During these volatile years, it's more
  important than ever to realize who your best friends really
  are. You're going to need them. . .and vice versa. So, who
  are you close to? Who knows you, inside and out? If you're

married, your spouse is surely your best friend. But, for this period of your life, you're going to need like-minded (and not so like-minded) women to see you through. If you're like many women these days, your e-mail box is filled with those goofy forwards from girlfriends. You know the ones. They espouse the value of friends, moms, sisters, and so forth. You know what? They're right! Your girlfriends—and the other women in your life—are the best cure for what ails you during the empty-nest years. Who else knows what you're going through? Who's there to wrap a sympathetic arm around your shoulder, or to listen to you tell and retell stories about your child's road trip to college? Your girlfriends, that's who. And this is the perfect opportunity to redefine your relationship with several of the women God has placed in your life. Perhaps it's time to mentor—or be mentored. At any rate, it's certainly time to reignite the flames of friendship. As you read Maggie's story, see if it doesn't touch your heart:

It's hard enough going through empty nest, but my story was even tougher. My husband left with another woman just as our youngest moved out on her own. Then, just a few months later, one of my parents died quite suddenly. This was a devastating time in my life. However, my friends—the women in my Bible study— swept in around me and literally walked me through that season. They were there when I needed arms around my neck. They were there to dry my tears. Honestly. . .I don't know where I would be without them. They are more than kindred spirits. . .they are my sisters.

- *Learning a new skill.* If you saw the movie *Shall We Dance?* perhaps you watched in awe as Richard Gere's character learned to ballroom dance. He waited until he was older to start something he'd secretly longed to do for years. And what about that old movie *City Slickers?* Remember those middle-aged men taking off on a Wild West adventure? Well, if they can do it, so can you! Don't let your age deter you! Many empty-nest moms dive into new hobbies and skills with abandon. You'll find them taking dance lessons, working out at the gym, learning to operate computers, joining photography clubs, and so on. There's just nothing like this season to get you excited about learning new things. So, what are you aching to learn? Always wanted to ski, but never knew how? No problem! Always wanted to quilt, but didn't have a clue? Perfect time to join a club. Always wanted to paint, but never picked up a brush? Grab one and head off to your local art class. In fact, you will find classes of all sorts at your local community college, so, what's holding you back? Dive in, Mom! The water's fine!

- *Volunteering.* Your children may no longer need you in the same way they used to, but that doesn't mean your days of helping are over. Turn those energies toward a worthy cause—or more than one if you're able. Volunteering, be it at a school, nursing home, or other civic or church-related organization, can not only fill your time but also take your mind off your current situation. And don't forget you're also making a difference—something not to be taken lightly! Take a look at Whitney's story:

As the mother of five, I took the empty-nest thing pretty hard. My kids and I had always spent a lot of time at the public library, so it was only natural that I volunteer there after they left. I now read stories to children every Monday afternoon. It's almost like going back in time, only I don't have to take the kids home with me, feed them, and put them down for the night!

◯ FLIGHT PATTERNS

Every woman has her own unique story. While one might
be interested in spicing up her marriage, another might be
fascinated with the idea of pursuing a hobby. One might like to
volunteer. Another might like to join an exercise class.

Take a look at some stories from women who've walked this
road. Maybe they will give you some ideas. Let's start with Patti:

> *I raised a houseful of kids, one right after the other. I
> loved every minute of it. When my second-to-youngest was
> leaving for college, I realized (with only one left at home)
> that I'd better start thinking about what I wanted to do
> once the last one was gone.*
>
> *For years, I'd loved to decorate. I re-did our house
> many times over through the years, and friends and
> family members often commented on how much they
> loved my color choices, my fabric choices, and so forth.
> I'd even helped several friends with their homes. Secretly,
> I'd always longed to be an interior decorator. Before my
> youngest ever left home, I got busy honing my craft. I took
> a couple of decorating classes and eventually connected
> with a friend who worked for a builder. They were
> looking for someone to decorate model homes.*
>
> *Model homes! This was a dream come true. I could
> hardly imagine having a blank slate that I could fill
> with color and texture. . .and at no cost to me! Not only
> that, I would be paid for my work. Over the next several
> months, as I worked my way through fabric samples,*

*paint chips, home décor stores, and more, I relished in
the fact that God—in His amazing way—had fulfilled a
lifelong dream, one I'd kept hidden for years. Talk about
a new lease on life!*

Dawn, another empty-nest mom, tells the following unique
story of how she and her husband redefined themselves after her
son moved out of the house.

> *Empty-nest status was thrust upon me early when
> my sixteen-year-old (my youngest) went for a visit with
> his natural father in Las Vegas, from whom we had been
> estranged for four years. My son called on my birthday
> and told me he wasn't coming home, that he was going to
> live with his father, a drug addict and alcoholic.*
>
> *I begged. I cried. I tried to cut deals. I contacted an
> attorney, a Christian man who called my son and my
> ex-husband and played go-between for the better part of
> a weekend. He finally called me and gave me some of the
> best advice I've ever received. "We could force the issue,
> go to court, drag it out, but at the end of the day, the
> judge is going to say he's old enough to choose. Let him go.
> Make sure he knows you love him and you support him,
> so when it goes south—and I think it will—he knows he
> has a safe place to come home to."*
>
> *So that's what I did. Then I moped around for about
> three days, crying, unhappy, totally unprepared for this
> next phase of life that had been thrust upon me far earlier
> than I expected. For about three days. That's how long it*

took my husband and me to realize, "Hey! We're alone! Woo-hoo! Let the honeymoon begin!"

I know God was in control of me. I did everything I could to rectify a situation I didn't think was right, but after I'd done everything I could, I had no choice but to relax and trust Him with my son's future, and with mine. It was the sweetest and most uncanny sense of peace you can imagine. I knew I was in His will, and He had the outcome in His hand.

That really was a new beginning for my husband and me. We'd married when my kids were small, so we'd never been alone. It really was like being honeymooners, only with the benefit of being with someone we already had a lot of history with. None of the awkward, getting-to-know-each-other moments. Just the joy of finally being alone with someone you dearly love.

Can you imagine walking a mile in Dawn's shoes? One part of her story that she didn't share (but one that's important to know) is that she began a new career at this juncture in her life. She not only watched God strengthen her marriage, she watched Him set her to flight in other areas of her life, as well.

And finally, there's Sally's story. Take a look at how her mother handled the empty-nest years:

I'm not an empty nester, but my mom was. I am the second of four biological kids, and when my younger sister was getting ready for college (leaving my mom with only one more in the house), she decided she wasn't ready to

be done being a mom yet and, long story short, ended up
adopting two more kids.

Whew! That last one might've thrown you for a loop. Not everyone feels led to start over again. But maybe, if you're missing being around kids, it's time to consider teaching a children's Sunday school class at your church or volunteering at your local children's hospital. There's nothing like being around kids to keep you young!

⟲ SMOOTH SAILING

> *Leaving home in a sense involves a kind of*
> *second birth in which we give birth to ourselves.*
> ANONYMOUS

Starting over after kissing the last child good-bye can be a challenge. So many things have—or will—be different. Where to start? With the Lord, of course. His Word will provide a respite from the unsettled feelings you have, and His people will be there to walk you through.

- *Therefore, I urge you, brothers, in view of God's mercy, to offer your bodies as living sacrifices, holy and pleasing to God—this is your spiritual act of worship. Do not conform any longer to the pattern of this world, but be transformed by the renewing of your mind. Then you will be able to test*

and approve what God's will is—his good, pleasing and
perfect will.
ROMANS 12:1–2 NIV

- *For which cause we faint not; but though our outward man*
  perish, yet the inward man is renewed day by day.
  2 CORINTHIANS 4:16 KJV

- *But they that wait upon the LORD shall renew their strength;*
  they shall mount up with wings as eagles; they shall run, and
  not be weary; and they shall walk, and not faint.
  ISAIAH 40:31 KJV

- *[The Lord] satisfies your desires with good things so that your*
  youth is renewed like the eagle's.
  PSALM 103:5 NIV

> *When I stand before God at the end of my life,*
> *I would hope that I would not have a single bit of*
> *talent left and could say, "I used everything you gave me."*
> ERMA BOMBECK

Chapter 3

DELIBERATE DOWNSIZING

*Cleaning your house while your kids are still growing
is like shoveling the walk before it stops snowing.*
PHYLLIS DILLER

BYE-BYE, BIRDIE

Remember that thing that happened when you were expecting a baby? They called it "nesting." Well, think of this phase of your life as "un-nesting." It's time to get rid of some of that stuff you acquired over the years, things that are cluttering your home, your workspace, and your mind.

Oy, the stuff! Wherever did it come from, and what are you supposed to do with it? If you're like most empty nesters, the garage or attic is lined with boxes and bins, filled with clothes, shoes, dolls, trinkets, posters, sports equipment, and other miscellaneous things belonging to your kids. And *then* there are the closets. Perhaps you're afraid to look inside them, for fear of what you'll find. (Or maybe you've already looked inside and feel completely overwhelmed!) What's a person to do with all of that . . .clutter? Keep it forever? Toss it all?

The truth is, all families—not just empty nesters—have stuff they should get rid of. Many hang on to those things because there's an emotional attachment. Others are overwhelmed and simply don't know where to start. Some take comfort in full rooms, a full garage, and a full attic, hoping to somehow fill the hole that's left after a child leaves the home. Others are eager to dump it all, claiming they have a right to every square inch of the house. Regardless of where you fit into this equation, it's likely you've got some de-junking to do. . .and perhaps not just in your home.

So, what does it mean to downsize? And how do you deal with the emotional stresses attached? Do you close your eyes and toss things out of the window, or do you take a more calculated approach? Do you let your heart get caught up in the process or throw caution to the wind? The answer is simpler than you might think.

Downsizing starts with an attitude. You've got to *want* to do it. (Turns out, this downsizing thing is more psychological than physical!) Some moms need to be convinced; others are more than ready. Regardless, you've got to reach the point where you're willing to let go of things. . .for your own sake. If you're having a hard time, just close your eyes and repeat: "I'm doing this for my own good! I'm doing this for my own good!"

And it's not just about "stuff." You're going to have to take a close look at a host of areas that require trimming back. Did you fill your day with activities when the kids were home? If so, you can now downsize your calendar (and all of the many things you would've written on it). Is your home too large? Maybe you'll want to downsize to a smaller one. Is your grocery budget overwhelming? Now you can trim back!

Of course, the "stuff" has to go, too! Do you find yourself with a full kitchen? Enough plates and silverware to feed an army? Time to put some things in storage. Is the garage loaded, top to bottom, with sports equipment you'll never use? Why not have a garage sale and make a little money? And what about those clothes. . .the ones the kids grew out of years ago but refused to give up? Have they left those things behind to clutter up your closets?

Yes, the empty-nest years are all about downsizing. But you're certainly not the first woman to have to trim back. Throughout time, women in your position have downsized. . . their homes, their stuff, their schedules, and much, much more.

And lest you think this is a new problem, think about Zipporah (Moses' wife) from the Old Testament. Can you imagine the look on her face when Moses said, "Honey, condense all of our belongings into a couple of bags. We're headed to the desert for forty years." What a challenge that must've been!

Downsizing requires careful strategizing. You don't want to go into it haphazardly. Some moms, in their zeal to get rid of things, toss out the baby with the bathwater. Others have a hard time letting go of just about everything! Even the smallest item is precious if it once belonged to a child!

Remember Gillian? She had a tough time with downsizing. Getting rid of her kids' stuff (to her way of thinking) was the equivalent of dishonoring the memories of all their good times together. But with her husband's help, they finally purged the house, packing away the things they thought the kids might still want later and shifting the other things around. In the end, they actually downsized to a new house. Who needed five bedrooms, after all? It was just the two of them and a miniature Schnauzer. (He didn't take up much space.)

In the end, Gillian adapted to her "shrinking" environment. In fact, she learned to love the new place. It didn't require as much housework. That freed her up to enjoy her new hobbies and to travel with her husband regularly. Only then could she see things in perspective.

What about you? Ready to meet the challenge? It's time to downsize, Mom. Time to trim back. Life has presented the perfect opportunity. . .so let's get packing!

SPREADING YOUR WINGS

Is it possible to make more of less? Do you find yourself losing not only a full nest but also all the activities that went with them? Sometimes losing the baggage gives you more to travel with. Don't believe it? It's true!

So, what are you downsizing? What areas of your life need to be trimmed?

- Schedules/daily activities

- Houses

- Kids' belongings

- Kitchenware

- Wardrobe

- Cars

- Grocery shopping, meals, and recipes

- Body

- Ministries

- Expectations

Whew! Are you tired, reading over that list? We probably could have listed many more, but let's start with these for now. If you're going to do this, you've got to have a plan. Grab a pen and paper. Jot down the things listed above, along with anything else that comes to mind. Don't go overboard, but try to think over every area you can. Then, after you read the next section, begin to write down a plan of action.

It's time to trim back, Mom. So, let's get crackin'!

◯ LIFTOFF!

Are you ready, Mom? Ready to de-junk? Ready to strike a balance between emotional attachment and de-cluttering? Sure, some of the items you're keeping are worth passing on to future generations. Others, however, are probably best served by passing them on to someone who might be able to use them. Try sifting through memories with an eye toward honoring them by giving the items new purpose in the hands of those who most need them.

As you downsize, there will be issues to address, both emotional and physical. Let's take a look at those concerns, one at a time.

- *Schedules/daily activities.* If you had to make a list of all the daily activities you used to do when your kids were at home, how long would the list be? Think of all the things you used to have to do! Carpooling, Little League games, piano lessons, school productions, choir rehearsals, etc. On and on the list goes. Most moms spend much of their week dealing with kid-related activities. Oh, but not the empty-nest mom! She's finally freed up to spend those hours doing the things she feels like doing. Instead of fretting over your empty (or near-empty) calendar, praise

God for it! And don't rush to fill the hours, not at first, anyway. Spend some time enjoying the peace and quiet, then slowly—ever so slowly—add to your own schedule as the Lord leads.

- *Houses.* Now that the kids are gone, you might be giving thought to moving to a smaller house. Many do. There are some great advantages to downsizing your home. A lower mortgage payment, for instance. And lower taxes. And now that you're clearing out some of the kids' stuff, you might not need the extra space. Perhaps you're like Laura, whose downsizing led her in a surprising direction:

> *Since childhood, I'd always loved the water. Trips to the lake and beach were highlights of my youth, but after marriage and three children I'd nearly forgotten how wonderful it was to awaken to the sound of the waves or the call of gulls. With plenty of time on our hands, my husband and I spent our anniversary at a bed and breakfast near a lake a short distance from our home. After spending three days boating, swimming, and generally enjoying the lake, neither of us wanted to go home. As soon as we could manage it, we arranged another weekend at the lake and then another. While driving back from a trip, my husband made the offhand comment that we could likely spend less if we just bought a home there. It was one of those moments that, when we look back, were pivotal. Within the year we'd bought a nice condo near the boat ramps. Suffice it to say we*

were highly motivated to spend as much time as we could there. Downsizing became an art form as we gradually moved those things we loved into the condo. Then came the opportunity for my husband to work at home rather than commute. Now we were really challenged. Why keep two homes if he didn't need to be near the office? But how to fit the rest of what we had into the condo? He and I discovered in short order that the only issue we had was how fast we could unload the unnecessary items that were keeping us from our goal of living full-time at the lake. What the kids didn't want I either donated or sold online. By Christmas we were at the lake in a smaller home with a much, much bigger life. Now I know I'll never let "stuff" keep me from what I really want. Who would?

- *Kids' belongings.* Ah, empty space! You now have some more room in your home with your teen away. It's yours to do with as you please. Sure, you want to be sensitive to your child's needs (and there are ways to include your kids in the trimming-down process), but here's the truth—the house is yours. You can do with it as you see fit. So, set your plans in motion. Figure out how you're going to trim back. What can be stored in the attic or garage and what can be tossed or sold in a yard sale? What have you been hanging on to as a crutch? Perhaps you can fill a small display case with your daughter's porcelain dolls or your son's baseball card collection. The rest? Well, it can be put into storage. Take a look at Missy's story. You'll probably get a kick out of it!

Not long after our boys graduated from college and moved out on their own, they came home to find us in the middle of a major remodeling project. We hadn't done much with our new home when we'd moved into it ten years before. We couldn't afford it with two and then three college tuitions. We were wallpapering, painting, re-carpeting. "How come you didn't do that when we were living here?" one of our sons asked. I just smiled. One day he'll understand.

Indeed. One day they will understand. . .when they are empty nesters themselves! In the meantime, enjoy that extra space!

- *Kitchenware.* Keep handy only what you need. Sometimes downsizing is simply a matter of moving things to a different location in your home. If you've got enough plates to feed an army but only use them once or twice a year, consider storing them on shelves in the garage or in the attic or basement. And, if you're like most moms, you've got enough silverware to fill several drawers. And plastic cups. And cereal bowls. Take inventory. Maybe it's time for a garage sale. You can make a little money by selling some of that stuff. Take a calculated approach, only selling what you're sure you won't need. But be honest with yourself. If you haven't used those Cinderella plates since your daughter was three, it's either time to toss them . . .or store them. Take a look at Carla's story:

I opened up the cupboard one day and several bowls

*fell out on my head. After coming to my senses, I realized
I needed to think about rearranging my kitchen. I started
by pulling everything—absolutely everything—out of the
cabinets and setting it onto the countertops. I quickly ran
out of room and had to use the kitchen table. That wasn't
enough space, so I ended up filling the dining room table,
too. It took me two hours just to unload everything. When
I finished, I was sweating! I realized, looking at all of the
stuff, that much of it—maybe half—hadn't been used in
years. I went to the garage for some empty boxes. I loaded
up the unusable stuff and donated it to a local charity.
Then I worked diligently to bring order out of chaos,
putting the remaining things away. Here's the funny part
. . .I don't miss any of that stuff. In fact, I didn't even
know half of it existed until that day!*

- *Wardrobe.* Your wardrobe is one of the first things you
  can look at trimming back when your kids are grown,
  especially if your children were involved in sports. Likely,
  you've got an abundance of team T-shirts and other
  school-themed clothing items you will never wear again.
  Consider having someone turn those T-shirts into a
  memory quilt for your sports star or cheerleader. What
  would have taken up space in a closet or dresser could
  become a gift with deep meaning and long-lasting charm.
  Or perhaps you can pass your collection on to someone
  on the team who has younger children. Likely she will be
  thrilled for the opportunity to cheer for the team without
  bankrupting her clothing budget.

- *Cars.* Perhaps you once needed a huge vehicle, but it's likely you can scale down now. You won't need as much seating anymore unless you're planning to travel with friends or take the kids on a summer vacation in between college semesters. Take a look at Cathy's story:

> *I drove a Suburban because it seated all six of us, plus friends. When my oldest got his license, we downsized to a six-passenger sedan (slightly smaller). Eventually, when the oldest three were gone and it was only my daughter and me, I bought a Mini Cooper. Talk about downsizing! Now I spend less on gas than I ever did while driving the family cars that preceded this one. The only thing that hasn't been reduced is the fun factor—a nice bonus indeed!*

- *Grocery shopping, meals, and recipes.* Grocery shopping can be quite a challenge when you're the mother of teenagers, but it can be a little stressful when the empty-nest years hit, too. Most women are used to buying things in quantity. Large bags of chicken. Big containers of this, that, and the other. Monstrous packages of toilet paper. And once the kids are grown, it takes awhile to get used to the idea that you can now buy smaller portions. Either that, or you can keep on buying larger portions and divvy them up. Consider Helen's story:

> *I always hated grocery shopping. It was a chore, something I never looked forward to. I'd done it so many hundreds of times that I had my grocery store memorized.*

I hardly had to think as I tossed things in the basket. My total at the register was always large, but with four kids to feed, whose wasn't? After my youngest daughter married, I lived alone. I found myself struggling at the grocery store. As I walked up and down the aisles, I'd reach for the "usual" stuff, then pause, remembering I didn't need it. At least, not in abundance. For a while I kept on buying in larger quantities, but when the food started going bad (and my refrigerator was overflowing with stuff I never touched) I finally decided to put an end to the madness. From that day until now, I've operated off of a menu. I only buy the ingredients I really need. Nothing gets wasted. Yes, it was a challenge, but I'm glad I did it. My pocketbook thanks me every time I go to the store!

- *Your body.* Have you given thought to the idea that this might be a good season to downsize your body? If you've spent the last few years with a pantry full of junk food (chips, cookies, sugary cereals, etc.) or have made a habit of heading to the drive-thru for dinner after soccer practice, it's somewhat likely you've put on a few pounds. Use this season to trim back on your calories and carbs, and watch what God does! He will strengthen you physically and walk alongside you as you shed a few of those unwanted inches. Perhaps this is the time to put in a small garden out back or join a food co-op. Not only will you have fresh produce and a slimmer figure, but you'll also downsize your grocery budget by growing your own.

- *Ministries.* Some moms are super-involved in their church while the kids are little. They teach Sunday school, help out in children's church, and work tirelessly to see that their kids have a great church experience. Maybe it's time to sit back for a while. To rest. To get your bearings. If the Lord wants you active in another ministry, He will open that door. In the meantime, catch your breath! And don't be so quick to volunteer for every little thing unless you truly feel the prompting of the Holy Spirit. Take a look at Lillian's story:

  I know that the empty-nest years are usually the perfect time to get involved at church, but that wasn't the case for me. After much thought and prayer, I actually decided this was the time to taper back on my church commitments. Why? I was exhausted! Over twenty years of involvement in every sort of ministry. My husband was the one who told me, "Enough is enough." So, we decided a sabbatical was in order!

- *Expectations.* Might sound a little odd, but one of the things you'll need to downsize is your expectations. Listen to Bridget's story:

  I always had great daydreams about my kids and what they would be like when they grew up. I also had great expectations for myself. My preconceived notions flew out of the window when both of my kids opted out of college. One became a delivery boy at a pizza place,

*then went on to become a franchise owner. The other
(who had always struggled with dyslexia) went on to be
certified to work with autistic children. She never spent a
day in a traditional classroom. By the time they were both
settled in their careers, I could see God's hand at work. I'd
"downsized" my expectations, sure, but He knew all along
what was right for my kids.*

Clearly, there are many areas you can consider downsizing during the empty-nest years. But remember, Mom. . .trimming back isn't a bad thing. And it's not just a practical thing. Eliminating waste from your life is the right thing to do.

FLIGHT PATTERNS

As we close out this chapter, let's take a look at three women who all chose to downsize in their own ways. Cathy's story is first:

> *I'm about to be an empty nester. Last of three will leave for college in August. I've recently found myself cleaning out cupboards and the freezer. For so many years I never had enough ketchup, salad croutons, vegetable oil, frozen pizza, etc. Now I'm backlogged as I kept buying but no one was here to use it all. Recently I've felt that I need to get rid of this excess; I don't need spare ketchup! I realized the other day that I'm doing the reverse of when a woman is pregnant and starts nesting—laying in supplies, making sure the cupboards are full, etc. So if that's called nesting, I think what I'm doing might be called "empty-nesting."*

The next story is from an empty nester named Lacey. Take a look at what she has to say about downsizing:

> *We deliberately downsized to sort of force the issue that our sons needed to be independent. We went from a big house to an RV as a "first step"—such a huge mistake in more ways than the size of this book would allow—foolish, selfish, unrealistic, and means of escape are the words that come immediately to mind to describe my actions during that time. But then we moved back*

*into a three-bedroom house in the city, then finally to
a one-bedroom cabin in the country. We love being out
in the country, but now that the boys' lives have settled
down, the small house makes it impossible to host holidays
or have them visit for even a short weekend. Within the
next five years, we plan to move to the state where the
boys live, and get a bigger house again—we have to have
room for eventual grandkids, and when we visit them
now, it just gets harder and harder to leave. I think the
empty nest has caused all of us to grow up!*

Finally, take a peek at author Grace Fox's story. Likely this
one will hit home:

*My husband and I recently discussed the fate of a
small homemade end table. "Let's take it to the thrift
store," he said. My heart sank. I couldn't justify keeping
it, but neither could I bear the thought of parting with
it. My father made it nearly fifty years ago; now he's
in a nursing home, paralyzed by a stroke and failing
physically. Disposing of the table felt wrong, like I was
throwing away a part of his legacy.*

*"I'm not ready to let it go," I said. "Can we wait
awhile? I just need some time to process this." Downsizing
from a rambling five-bedroom home to a three-bedroom
townhouse prompted many similar conversations. Moving
meant trading a spacious storage room and a double
carport for limited storage space under the stairwell and
a single carport that came with strata rules—no bikes, no*

barbecues, no boxes allowed.

With only thirty days to make our transition, we began sorting and whittling, stupefied by how much a family could accumulate. The process left us exhausted physically, but it was worth the effort. [44]

SMOOTH SAILING

Downsizing can be a challenge, but you're up for that challenge! Make yourself a promise that the Lord will be at the center, and everything else will fall into place. You'll find soon enough that He will not only guide your efforts to cut back but will also give you peace, joy, and even an excitement that surpasses all understanding.

Take a look at these scriptures:

- *"You're blessed when you're at the end of your rope. With less of you there is more of God and his rule."*
  MATTHEW 5:3 MSG

- *"You're blessed when you're content with just who you are—no more, no less. That's the moment you find yourselves proud owners of everything that can't be bought."*
  MATTHEW 5:5 MSG

---

[4] "Surviving the Downsizing Dilemma," Grace Fox, *Focus on the Family* (used with permission).

- *For instance, we know that when these bodies of ours
  are taken down like tents and folded away, they will be
  replaced by resurrection bodies in heaven—God-made, not
  handmade—and we'll never have to relocate our "tents"
  again. Sometimes we can hardly wait to move—and so we
  cry out in frustration. Compared to what's coming, living
  conditions around here seem like a stopover in an unfurnished
  shack, and we're tired of it! We've been given a glimpse of the
  real thing, our true home, our resurrection bodies! The Spirit
  of God whets our appetite by giving us a taste of what's ahead.
  He puts a little of heaven in our hearts so that we'll never
  settle for less.*
  2 CORINTHIANS 5:1–5 MSG

Chapter 4

DEALING WITH THE BIG "D" (DEPRESSION)

How then can we account for the persistence of the myth that inside the empty nest lives a shattered and depressed shell of a woman—a woman in constant pain because her children no longer live under her roof? Is it possible that a notion so pervasive is, in fact, just a myth?

LILLIAN BREWLOW RUBIN

◖ BYE-BYE, BIRDIE

Somehow, somewhere, the story got started. Oh, you know the
one. . .the one that says every empty-nest mom must go through
a grieving spell when the house empties. That she will weep
and wail and feel that her sole purpose for existing has just left
the house. While it is true that most women agonize over their
children leaving, not all do. Some take it in stride and get on
about the business of living. Others actually look forward to the
day the last one takes flight and celebrate it happily. Not all have
it that easy, though. Some really do struggle, trying to figure out
their new "role." They need time to adjust.

What about you, Mom? Are you a take-it-all-in-stride kind
of person, or someone who agonizes over major life-shifts? If
you're tempted to get too down about it all, you might actually
find yourself sinking into depression. Some women get caught in
this trap and struggle to find their way out.

According to the *Psychology Today* Web site:

> *Empty Nest Syndrome refers to feelings of depression,
> sadness, and/or grief experienced by parents and caregivers
> after children come of age and leave their childhood
> homes. This may occur when children go to college or
> get married. Women are more likely than men to be
> affected; often, when the nest is emptying, mothers are
> going through other significant life events as well, such as
> menopause or caring for elderly parents. Yet this doesn't
> mean that men are completely immune to Empty Nest
> Syndrome. Men can experience similar feelings of loss*

regarding the departure of their children. [5]

Some mothers can't get beyond the feeling that their sole purpose in existing is to take care of their kids. Now, the children have moved on. The family has been rocked. "Normal" isn't normal anymore. Mom and Dad are faced with a sudden shift in the earth. Somebody's missing. One child. . .or maybe two, three, or four. For these women, depression can become more than just a syndrome. It can become a deep, dark well, one they have trouble climbing out of.

If you're feeling despondent or your emotions continue to get in the way—for example, you cry at the drop of a hat, you have trouble focusing on other things, you turn to food or shopping for comfort, you feel like giving up or have other feelings of worthlessness—it's probably time to consider seeking professional help. A Christian counselor can give you the tools you need to make it through this season. If you're reluctant to open up and share what you're feeling, prayerfully consider doing it anyway. God can and will use wise counsel to pull you up from even the deepest well. The Holy Spirit—your ultimate Comforter—can lift both your head and your heart.

This is also a great time to lean on friends who've walked a mile in your shoes. Perhaps this is one of the reasons the Bible makes it clear that older women should counsel the younger ones. We need the advice and counsel of women who've walked this road before us. We can learn from their mistakes and possibly avoid making a few ourselves. This is also a great time

---

[5] *Psychology Today Diagnosis Dictionary*, s.v. "Empty Nest Syndrome," http://www.psychologytoday.com/conditions/emptynest.html, (accessed April 22, 2009).

to have some heart-to-heart discussions with your spouse, if you have one. If anyone knows what you're feeling, he does. In fact, he might just be struggling, too.

There are so many ways to get beyond depression. Exercise helps. Eating right, too. Staying busy. Taking up a hobby. These are all good things. But, ultimately, it comes down to your "altar time." Running to God (who knows your heart) is truly the best way to see your way through the valley of depression.

Let's take a look at a familiar verse from The Message: "Birds find nooks and crannies in your house, sparrows and swallows make nests there. They lay their eggs and raise their young, singing their songs in the place where we worship. GOD-of-the-Angel-Armies! King! God! How blessed they are to live and sing there!" (Psalm 84:3–4).

The key to staying strong is to build your nest near the altar of God. If you raised your children to believe in Him, there's no reason you need to move your nest from that safe place, now that the kids have moved on. In fact, it's more important than ever that you draw close, particularly if you're struggling emotionally.

Let's look at how Gillian handled the bout with depression that she walked through when her kids left home. She'd given so much of herself to others over the years that she hardly knew how to "do life" with her own needs in mind. At times, she felt very alone—like a lonely bird sitting on a tree limb, trying to figure out her reason for existence.

She managed to do pretty well around her friends, so much so that many of them didn't even realize she was depressed. But her husband knew. And her best friend. They talked to her about the things they saw—the weight loss, the circles under her eyes, the sadness in her countenance. She dove into activities, thinking busyness would somehow ease the pain, but it did not. Sure, it numbed the ache somewhat, but not permanently. No, for that, she needed something else entirely.

Ultimately, she found a godly counselor who led her to Psalm 84:3–4. He encouraged her to take a look at the reality of her pain. She didn't want to do it at first. Who would? Calling a spade a spade isn't always easy. Eventually Gillian came to grips with the fact that she was, indeed, hurting. With the counselor's help, and through the power of the Holy Spirit, she began to make a concerted effort to stay close to the altar of God, to trust Him with her emotions and her pain. Like the little sparrow on the tree limb, she began to see her value to God, not as a mom, but as a daughter of the King. She grew to lean on the verse, "Are not two sparrows sold for a cent? And yet not one of them will fall to the ground apart from your Father" (Matthew 10:29 NASB). Gillian began to recognize who she was as a child of the King.

Truly, the only way to find your way out of the pit is to see yourself the way God sees you. You are precious and valuable to Him, and He wants to see you walking in the fullness of your potential. That often requires taking a good—sometimes intense—look at the things you're dealing with, from the inside out. So, hang on, Mama Bird! We're about to travel to the depths. . .so that we can eventually soar to the heights!

SPREADING YOUR WINGS

If joy were the only emotion God intended us to feel,
He could just zap us and take us to heaven right now. . . .
The truth is that our trials are a furnace forging us into gold.

BARBARA JOHNSON

True depression involves a sadness that goes beyond the norm. It often causes the person to withdraw, from both friends and family. And depression is usually secondary to some sort of trauma. It can shake you to the core, but the "trigger" for depression is really where you need to go to find answers. If you're wrestling with feeling "down" much of the time, take a look at the following list to see where the trouble began.

What are you struggling with, Mom? Do any of these things sound familiar?

- Lack of purpose

- A big, clean, empty house

- A husband who's given over to his career

- Loss and grief

- Abrupt change in schedule

- Sense of anticipation gone

- Kids coming back from school, but not to see you

- Relationship problems related to your depression

- "No one understands what I'm going through"

- Switching from "teacher" to "student"

- Change of life times two

- Kids who leave under bad circumstances/things not good/ feeling like a failure

Do you see now that your depression could very well be linked to one of these things listed above? The key to getting rid of depression—along with seeking God and getting wise counsel—is to go all the way back to the beginning and seek out its root. You can mask the symptoms, but if you don't do business with God about the real issue, you won't be truly healed. And what would be the point of pretending? No, it's time to do business with the Lord so that you can walk in freedom and wholeness!

C LIFTOFF!

Now that you've taken a look at the various things that can trigger depression, let's look at how to address them, one by one. However, let's start with a word of caution. These suggestions aren't meant to be a cure-all. This book is not meant to offer a professional opinion. These are simply thoughts and ideas to assist you in your journey toward walking in health. If your depression is deep, please seek the help of a counselor or pastor. And, as much as you are able, guard your mind and heart against depression. Take your thoughts captive (otherwise you're dragging all the junk with you when you travel).

Focus on the words found in 2 Corinthians 10:4–5: "For the weapons of our warfare are not carnal but mighty in God for pulling down strongholds, casting down arguments and every high thing that exalts itself against the knowledge of God, bringing every thought into captivity to the obedience of Christ" (NKJV). If your thoughts are truly His thoughts, then they will be encouraging, positive.

With that in mind, let's take another look at that list:

- *Lack of purpose.* Have you always defined yourself as "the mom of" someone? If so, then you're probably feeling a little lost without the kids around. First you've got to come to grips with who you are in Christ. You are His beloved, His daughter, His child. Your Daddy is the King of kings and Lord of lords and He gave His very life for you. You were created to praise Him, and to make His praises glorious! Your purpose for existing is to love and be loved.

87

And then, of course, to share that love with others so that all might know! Sure, you raised your kids. You poured into their lives and did a fine job, at that. But there are plenty of other people out there who need your love, your encouragement, and your friendly smile.

- *A big, clean, empty house.* Are you struggling with a clean, empty house? Do you often wonder why it bothers you so much? Take a look at Jeanene's story. Likely you can relate.

> *I was always one of those people who said, "I will be happy when (fill in the blank)." With four kids to raise, my house was often messy. One of the things I most looked forward to was a clean, organized house. Then—finally!—the last child left the house and I was able to whip it into shape. Held some appeal for a time. Then, ironically, I began to long for the mess. I found myself leaving things scattered about. . .on purpose. Just because. It depressed me to live in total cleanliness, because it was a constant reminder of what I'd lost.*

Are you like Jeanene? Struggling because you got what you wanted, only to realize that wasn't what you needed at all? While it might not be a great idea to scatter things about on purpose—especially if you or your spouse tend to ignore what's underfoot—it may be a good idea to consider why you're missing this stage of your life. Perhaps a messy house is the outward sign of the life you think is behind you. If it's a full house you're wanting, consider turning the problem over to God and allowing Him to use your home for His purposes. Who knows? You might end up hosting a Bible study or book club meeting or even becoming a foster parent. Maybe offering up that spare bedroom to house visiting missionaries is what the Lord will ask of you. Go ahead and make the offer, then wait in joyful anticipation of what will happen. We serve such a creative God. Who knows what He will come up with to solve your dilemma? Rest assured, however, that He will!

- *A husband who's given over to his career.* If you're like most women, you spent the last eighteen years putting the children and their numerous needs and activities ahead of yours. So who can blame husbands who are now totally dedicated to their career? Yet now is the time for both of you to take a big step back from "the way things were" to "the way things can be." Look for ways to enjoy each other. Plan date nights. Purchase some new lingerie. Redo your bedroom. Don't drive him crazy with your antics, but let him know you're there for him. And don't let depression rear its head if he doesn't always respond favorably. It's going to take him awhile to shift gears, too. And he might be turning to his work for comfort. Chances are, he misses the kids, too.

- *Loss and grief.* In some ways, going through empty-nest syndrome is like going through a death. You have to allow yourself time and space to grieve. And you can't rush through the process. On the other hand, if it appears you're remaining "down" for too long, it might be time to take inventory. Sometimes you just need to move forward to the next level in the grieving process. Let's take a look at Marla's story:

My mother went into a deep depression when I, her "baby," left home. I saw that and determined at that time that I was going to develop interests that would provide a full life once I was no longer parenting full-time. Over the life of my children I consciously developed interests that could blossom more fully once they were gone. I made a written list, and now that I have only one child living at home part-time (summers when not in college), that list is providing abundance and joy in my new life as an empty nester.

- *Abrupt change in schedule.* Empty nesters often go from being overwhelmingly busy to having no schedule. It's a lifestyle and suddenly it's gone and you don't know what to do with your time. First take a deep breath and thank God for allowing that busyness to end and for ushering you into a season of peace and quiet. Sometimes the loss of the familiar can overshadow the blessing of the present. Those who were stay-at-home moms often have a tough time with this, though most were used to switching gears from the office to the hockey rink or soccer field. If it's the schedule you're lacking, then put yourself on one. Sit down with the Lord and ask Him to create a daily plan. Set times for tasks such as exercise, meal preparation, etc. Don't forget to add in an hour for meeting with Him and, if you can manage it, at least one long soak in a tub full of bubbles for yourself! If you let Him, God will fill your calendar. Once you have a plan, stick to it!

- *Sense of anticipation gone.* You've spent the better part of the last eighteen-plus years with a constant sense of anticipation. You could hardly wait for your baby to learn to walk. Then you anticipated her first day at school. That anticipation mounted once again when she learned to drive, started high school, and graduated in her cap and gown. If your child is off at school (or married), it's likely you're feeling a bit of a let-down. It's kind of like after-birth blues. On the surface, it may seem there's nothing to look forward to. Oh, but there is! Now you can begin to look forward to the things God is soon to bring about in your life! Get ready, Mom! Great things are coming!

- *Kids coming back from school, but not to see you.* Here's Kim's take on the issue:

    My boys were coming in from college and I was ecstatic! I made plans—dinner, their favorite dessert, and a movie—but they said, "Sorry, Mom. Hanging out with [my friends] tonight." I was devastated! Here's another conundrum. . .while my sons are away at school, they generate laundry, which they bring home. It stays while they go out. While I'm home doing their laundry, they're out having a great time. Coming home after the last dryer load has stopped is the norm on the weekends they're in

> *town. I find I miss them as much when they're home as I*
> *do when they're away at school. And yet I don't want to*
> *make an issue of it because I'm afraid I'll never see them.*

Sound familiar, Mom? Do you face the same thing, or perhaps some variation of it? Do you suffer in silence as Kim did? If so, you must be honest with your children. If a situation such as Kim's is breaking your heart, don't let it continue. It's likely your children have no clue they are hurting you. Perhaps now is the time to begin new traditions, maybe a meal together on Sunday after church or a special Saturday lunch cooked outside on the grill. Anything that will give your kids the heads-up that you want to connect with them even as you recognize they also want to see their friends. Or, especially if you're suffering from the clean-house syndrome mentioned earlier, encourage your kids to entertain at your home. Rather than going to "hang out" elsewhere, have them stay and watch the big game at your place. Offer to order pizzas for the group. You never know how much fun a group of kids can be until you've done without them in your home for a while.

- *Relationship problems related to your depression.* Chances are, for many years now the main topic of conversation between you and your spouse has been the children. The baby updates started well before the birth of child number one, when he or she kicked, hiccoughed, and generally made sleeping impossible. Then came infanthood, which quickly became the preteen years, the teen years, and finally the empty nest. Now that the last moving box is safely in the hands of your son or daughter and the house is empty, what is there to talk about with your spouse? Unlearning years of "kid conversation" might not be easy, but it certainly can be done. For instance, when you're tempted to comment about how long it's been since Junior called, why not ask your husband about his day instead? Or maybe you can inquire about his job, his golf game, or even his opinion on the latest headlines. Ask open-ended questions rather than ones that can be answered with a yes or no or, worse, with a grunt. Still stuck for things to do now that the kids are gone? Perhaps a trip back down memory lane to your honeymoon years is in order. Remember when there were no distractions? When it was just you and your husband and the twinkle in his eye? Why not revisit those days? Because it is just you and your husband, perhaps it is time to cause that twinkle to return. After all, the entire house is yours.

- *"No one understands what I'm going through."* Clearly, God does! Remember, He sent His only Son "out of the nest," so to speak. And you are probably surrounded by empty nesters on all sides, though some cope better than others. However, if you still need someone to talk to about your thoughts, your feelings, why not journal? Take a look at Leigh's story. It might give you some ideas:

   I have always been shy. I'm definitely not the kind of person who opens up and talks to strangers. So, when I began to feel "down" about my nest emptying, I bought a journal and chronicled my thoughts. I wrote down the sad things, the angry things, the funny things, the quirky things. Whenever one of the kids would do something special for me, I'd write it down. Whenever the Lord would answer a prayer, I'd write it down. Before long, my "empty nest" journal turned into something else entirely! It became more of a prayer and praise journal. I've now filled several of those little books. It's interesting to go back and read the first ones, to see how far I've come. I truly believe that writing is cathartic. Cleansing. It's good for the soul, especially the empty-nest mom's soul.

- *Switching from "teacher" to "student."* You've spent much of your adult life pouring into others, it's true. You've played the role of teacher for years. Now, instead of being in charge and being someone with the answers, it's more likely you're floundering like a fish out of water. You don't know where your boundaries are anymore. Here's the truth, Mom. You now have to learn how to let go. You are currently a student in a class that you never signed up for. You might not get passing grades at first, either. You have to let your kids make their own decisions regardless of the pitfalls you know are there. If and when you do give advice, you must be cautious in your approach so as not to be seen as trying to run their lives or live yours through them. You have to trust that the things you taught them are still there and that they will make good decisions. You know what you taught them, you know the values you instilled in them. Remember the promises of God about how if you train them up right, when they are old they will not depart from it (Proverbs 22:6). That doesn't necessarily mean they won't stray at first, but hang in there. God has a plan for their lives. Your role is changing. It's like when they were learning to swim. . .you had to let go so they could see they were able to do it on their own. You were still there, of course, but they were keeping themselves afloat.

- *Change of life times two.* If you're like many women, the empty-nest years have hit at about the same time you're walking through perimenopause or menopause. Talk about an overload of emotions! Your hormones are off. You feel like weeping much of the time, but can't really put your finger on the reason. If the mood swings are bad, talk to your doctor. Get out and walk. Exercise releases endorphins, which will help to level off any depression. Do things with other women: walking, shopping, lunches, dinner, Bible study, movies. If you have a spouse, do things with him. Seek out others who've dealt with empty-nest syndrome and menopause simultaneously, and ask for their input. You aren't alone. And there is light on the other side of this.

- *Kids who leave under bad circumstances/things not good/ feeling like a failure.* In situations like these, you can feel totally helpless. You long for your child but you don't have a relationship with her. You worry that out of her anger, she may make rash, harmful choices that will have repercussions for her for a lifetime. Your mind wanders to your son all day long. You blame yourself, you blame your spouse, you even blame the child. Often there are so many words you wish you had not said, so many words you wish you had said. You wonder if he is lost to you forever. Talk to God, tell Him all your concerns; He knows you and your child. Be available for your child should he make any attempt at communication or contact. Be willing to go to a counselor with or without the child. When you do hear from him, let him know you love him. God loves us unconditionally, Jesus died for us while we were still sinners. And remember, He who began a good work in your child is faithful to complete it. That son or daughter is being wooed by the Lord, even now. As much as you are able, be kind, tenderhearted, and truthful but foremost show love at all times, even if it's tough love (and there may be times when tough love is the only option). Ultimately, God is judge. You were put here to guide your children until adulthood and love them always. God knows how to mold them and use their circumstances to bring them back into your family and into God's family. Before we move on, let's take a look at Lilly's story.

My oldest (a girl) was easy. She graduated at the top of her class and never gave us a minute's trouble. But when my youngest (a boy) graduated, I knew we were headed for a rocky road. Drugs. Alcohol. DWI. Time in jail. We went through it all. We had to make a decision that wasn't easy . . .to kick him out of the house. It took years of wandering on his part. There was even a time when he was living in his car. Still, I kept praying and kept believing God would restore my son, both to Himself and to the family. There were times when my heart broke for him. I wanted to sweep him back into the fold and shower him with grace. My husband had other ideas, so we stuck with the tough love approach. It took several years, but my son is now healed and whole. He's happily married with two children and is a great husband and father. No more drugs. No more alcohol. He's clean and sober. Thank God for the courage to exhibit tough love when necessary!

FLIGHT PATTERNS

Different women display symptoms of depression differently. With some, you would never know. Others? You can't seem to pull them from the depths, even if you try. Don't try to put yourself into a box if you're struggling with depression, and whatever you do, don't compare yourself to others. Every situation is different. And your response to it might have to be just as different!

As we wrap up this section on depression, let's take a look at a couple of women who struggled with it firsthand. We'll start with Abby.

I have firsthand experience in dealing with the Big "D." It's not fair when menopause, an empty nest, and a cross-country move all happen at once! Menopause interrupts your ability to sleep, so you are left to deal with stress on half a battery. Without the kids to give structure to your life, you begin to flounder trying to figure out who you are and what to do with all the free time.

You move and at fifty plus years of age it's harder to make new friends than it was when you were younger. And I wonder why I was depressed? In that tired, stressed environment, old hurts and grievances start coming up out of the place they've been stuffed for years and soon you just can't cope with it all. But God provided help in the form of a caring nurse practitioner and a Christian counselor.

Psalm 23 says that God will be with us through the shadow and He is ever faithful. It was a struggle, but through it all God drew me ever closer to Him, and my relationships with God, husband, and sons have never been better.

Now let's look at another story. See if you can relate:

I was so sad when my oldest daughter packed her bags and left to go to Tyler, Texas, to study at YWAM (Youth with a Mission). As she packed her car, I had mixed emotions, thinking how happy I was for my daughter, so grown up and out to Bible School. But when she was gone I walked inside the house, took a look at her bedroom, and sat at her bed, thinking, She is not coming back. Then a few years later our son did the same thing.

It hit me like a rock! My babies are not coming back. This is it!

I cried and cried, but the worst feeling that I had was realizing the responsibility God had given me as a mother (having the children, training them in the ways of the Lord) had ended. Right?

No! It was the beginning of a new era in their lives and ours. Then, my soul emptied out as my heart searched the heart of God, saying, "God, did I accomplish the task You gave to me as a mother? How did I do? Did I pass the test? O Lord, I pray that whatever I did, whether it was right or wrong, whether I accomplished Your will in my children's lives, I pray that You use every word, every correction, every teaching I gave my children about You. That my kids never remember the bad and the ugly of our lives but the seed that my husband and I planted in their hearts about You."

We're going to end with one more story. Perhaps you can relate to this mom's struggle.

My daughter left home in 1994 to attend college. As a single mom of an only child, depression walloped me. I remember sitting on my stairs, crying as though my child had died. The Lord brought to mind a friend whose son had died earlier that summer—I felt not shame, but maybe an understanding of how fortunate I was. Quickly I discovered college lasts only six months, and Sarah was home a lot until she married.

Can you relate to that kind of grieving? Many women do go through intense, agonizing spells when their children leave. There's no denying it. But when the "spell" lasts too long or goes too deep, it's time to seek help. You need to figure out what is "normal depression" and when it's gone too far. There are truly times when you need the assistance of a counselor or psychologist. And don't forget that the Holy Spirit's role is to bring comfort. He will surround you with peace, if you let Him. And guard yourself from the enemy's schemes during this volatile season. Don't let depression zap you of your dreams for the future. . .or your faith.

SMOOTH SAILING

Change is hard, but when the change feels like loss instead of a new season, it can be particularly difficult. Make no mistake, depression is real and should be taken seriously when the sadness you feel becomes overwhelming. In contrast, if what you're feeling is a case of the blues brought on by losing the familiar days of messy kitchens, rushed breakfasts, and after-school miles in the carpool lane, then rest assured that acknowledging the issue means you're well on your way to solving it. Just look at what God's Word says about His prescription:

- *Why are you downcast, O my soul? Why so disturbed within me? Put your hope in God, for I will yet praise him, my Savior.* PSALM 42:5 NIV

- *Worry weighs us down; a cheerful word picks us up.*
  PROVERBS 12:25 MSG

- *A cheerful heart brings a smile to your face; a sad heart makes it hard to get through the day.*
  PROVERBS 15:13 MSG

- *For thou art my lamp, O LORD: and the LORD will lighten my darkness.*
  2 SAMUEL 22:29 KJV

Chapter 5

Free Time—A Gift from God

*You know your children have grown up when they stop asking you
where they came from and refuse to tell you where they are going.*
UNKNOWN

◯ BYE-BYE, BIRDIE

Don't you love it when people ask that age-old question, "If money were no object and you could go anywhere in the world you wanted, where would you go and why?" In this chapter, we're going to ask a similar question: if you had the *time* to do whatever you really wanted, what would you do. . .and why?

Ah, time! It's that illusive thing we dream about when our kids are young. Somewhere between changing diapers, mopping floors, rushing to work, fixing dinner, doing laundry, and scrubbing toilets, that is. "If I just had the time, I would. . ." (Wouldn't it be fun to fill in this blank?) We dream of a day when we can spend leisurely hours at the beach or go to lunch with a friend and not be interrupted by a frantic phone call from a kid with a need. Perhaps those days are closer than you think.

Your children are grown now, Mom, and it's likely you have more time on your hands than before. Oh, I know, I know. . . some of you are saying, "Are you serious? My days are fuller now than ever!" Well, congratulations! You've already made the jump. You're living your life to the fullest, trying new things, exploring new possibilities. You are a beacon for others to do the same. Some, however, are still scrambling, trying to figure out how to fill their days, to make the best use of their hours. It is for those who are asking, "Now what?" that this chapter was written.

Think of this season as a diving board. You're standing at the end, bouncing up and down, about to make that fateful leap over the edge into the water below. The what-ifs are endless. Still, you've got mixed feelings. You miss the kids. You want to start exploring possibilities for your own life, but you're scared. Is it really okay to be this self-focused?

Here's the truth, Mom. Unless you take care of you. . .unless you're healthy, fulfilled, and emotionally secure. . .you won't have much to give to others. And part of the journey includes finding out *who* you are and what you like to do. How you would fill the hours if you didn't have to factor in kids and kid stuff. Interesting question, right?

Before you can answer that, however, it's good to recognize one simple fact: you have always lived for others. Now, it's just you and the Lord (or you, your spouse, and the Lord). Your days used to be filled with PTA meetings, carpooling, sport practices, music lessons, and so forth. And while those were great ways to spend your hours, they were 100 percent focused on your kids. Now your focus is shifting and you get to think about what *you* want to do. And, no, that's not a selfish thing. . .at least, it doesn't have to be. It's a realistic, practical thing. . .one meant to keep you healthy and strong in the Lord.

Gillian, a stay-at-home mom, was filled with ideas for how to fill her free time when the kids went off to school. She'd always wanted to paint, for instance. But who had time? The only paintings in her world were those hanging on the refrigerator door. And she longed to travel. Most of the family trips had been to places not of her choosing. Now she could make the leap. And leap she did!

The year after her youngest left for college, Gillian and her husband finally took that trip to Italy they'd been talking about for years! And she signed up for an art class at her local community college, too. Gillian's husband was overly busy during this season of his life. He'd finally worked his way up the corporate ladder and was enjoying success at work. But that meant he couldn't devote as much time to Gillian as she'd hoped. Instead of moaning about that fact, she took on a part-time job and paid extra-special attention to her hubby during the time they did have together.

What about you, Mom? Looking for ideas to fill your time? If you're floundering, then consider talking things through with other empty nesters. They have already walked this road before you and know what you're facing. They will be loaded with ideas, too!

One last thought before closing out this section. Free time is a good thing. But it's not always critical to fill it. You might consider actually taking some time for yourself. Get a massage. Meditate on the Word. Take a bubble bath. Listen to worship music. Take pictures of flowers. Pray. Relax. Enjoy the respite from life's craziness! If you get too busy, you might miss some of the messages the Lord is trying to whisper in your ear.

Time is not your enemy, Mom. Though it seems to be marching by in a hurry, it's an invitation to join the dance of life.

C SPREADING YOUR WINGS

So, you're looking for great ways to fill your time. Here are just a few:

- Increase your prayer and devotion time.
- Travel.
- Get caught up on mammograms, Pap smears, physicals, etc.
- Take a class.
- Spice up your marriage.
- Adopt a pet.

Here are some not-so-great ways to fill your time:

- Read books with questionable content.
- Watch too much television.
- While away hours on the Internet.
- Focus on yourself.
- Drive your husband or children crazy with unnecessary attention.
- Worry.
- Get into other people's business.

◖ LIFTOFF!

Time is a precious commodity. It's never a good thing to waste it (though it's always good to take a Sabbath rest when your work is through). Let's take another look at that list above. There are plenty of ways to fill your days with fun and enjoyment.

- *Increase your prayer and devotion time.* By far the healthiest thing you can do with your spare time is to increase your Bible reading and prayer time. If you've always rushed through this, slow down and take a deep breath. Don't make it a works-based thing: "I have to do this at a certain time every day or I'm a bad Christian." Just commune with the Lord. Pray the psalms! Worship with some of your favorite songs. Spend time on your knees in prayer. Mix it up! Don't make it about rules. Make it about relationship. Take a look at what Chassie did:

> *I've always been the sort of person to run a hundred miles an hour. I did it when the kids were home and I do it now, years later! My prayer time was usually rushed or neglected altogether. I promised the Lord—and myself— that I would take half an hour in the morning. It was hard at first. But then I started worshipping to music. The music caused me to want to open the Bible. And the Bible. . .well, I learned that I can actually pray the scriptures. This was a revolutionary concept. I started with Psalm 139. I'd read a scripture, then pause to pray. . .whatever came to mind as a result of what I'd read. This is such a precious time to*

me now. Doesn't feel like a chore at all! It's worth slowing down for!

Isn't that an awesome idea? Perhaps you could try praying the scriptures, as well. Anything to get you out of a rut is a good thing!

- *Travel.* What do you say, Mom? Have you always longed to travel? Where would you go, if you could? Even if money is an object (and for most it is), you can still travel to local places—museums, theaters, the countryside, arboretums, and so forth. Think of all the many places close to home where you can set out on an adventure! And if you're interested in "serious" traveling (say, a trip to Paris), begin to plan now. Open a bank account with that trip in mind. Begin to acquire travel brochures. Research hotels and bed-and-breakfasts. Your dream will only become a reality if you step out and actually make it happen!

- *Get caught up on mammograms, Pap smears, physicals, etc.* This is a great way to spend your time, particularly if you're behind on any of these things. If you're over fifty, make sure you have a colonoscopy, as well. Perhaps you're like Sandy who didn't miss a checkup. Good thing. She felt fine and yet that one mammogram she took as a result of her yearly physical saved her life—literally. There on the film was a mass so tiny her monthly check had failed to note it. Sandy's story is a positive one: a year later she's free of cancer and shouting to the world that ignoring your yearly checkups is foolish. Listen, dear one! The life you save may be your own—and you've got so much more to do!

- *Take a class.* We covered this in a previous chapter, but search through the catalog from your local community college. You'll be stunned at all of the classes it offers. You might try something totally random—pottery, for instance. Or voice lessons. Who knows? The possibilities are endless. You will find that your local hardware stores offer classes, too (faux painting, etc.)! Think outside the box.

- *Spice up your marriage.* Oh, what fun! Your husband will appreciate this one. Begin to think of all the ways you can spice up your marriage. And, no, this isn't all sexual. Start by implementing a date night. Then give some thought to redecorating your bedroom and bathroom, using plenty of candles and other romantic elements. Pack "I love you" notes in your husband's lunch. Give him a massage after a long day at work. In short, begin to think like a honeymooner again! (Let's be honest. . .if we really thought like honeymooners, it would change pretty much everything!)

- *Adopt a pet.* Many women who swore off pets when their kids were growing end up pet lovers after the fact. There's nothing like a fluffy little canine (or a purring kitty) to make things right with the world. If you decide to adopt a pet, choose carefully! You need a breed that fits your lifestyle. Perhaps you're moving from a big home to a small one. Consider a smaller pup over ones who'll grow into their enormous paws. Traveling? Do you want a fish instead? Or maybe you'll need to make do with visiting the grand-dogs. Take a look at Marlene's story:

> *Just before my youngest two daughters got married, I got a miniature dachshund, a female named Sasha. She was quite a handful, but I loved her! Then, so that she wouldn't get lonely, I got another minidachshund, this one a male. I named him Copper. Once the kids left home, these little dogs became my constant companions. They filled my days with antics (some good and some bad). They even slept with me at night. (I'm single, so no one complained.) To this day, they bring me great joy and comfort. And they're great for scaring away would-be bad guys! They yap like great big dogs whenever someone rings the doorbell!*

Not-so-great ways to fill your time:

Now we're going to take a hard look at some time-consuming habits that might not be healthy—spiritually or emotionally. We'll start with a popular one (one many women won't confess to!).

- *Read books with questionable content.* Okay, let's be honest. Many women, even Christian women, get caught up in those not-so-great romance novels. Oh, not the Christian ones. You know the ones. Steamy. Exotic. They take you to far-off places and introduce you to Fabian, with his long-flowing hair and rippled six-pack. Through the pages of the story, he wines and dines you, then sweeps you—and your imagination—away to places you really don't need to be going. If you're truly honest with yourself, those books hold you captive for more than one reason. They're titillating and often fill a void—albeit in a wrong way. If you've never given thought to your reading material before, please do so now. What you read should be glorifying to God and should point you toward Him. There are some awesome Christian book clubs (heartsongpresents.com, for instance). These books offer the same exciting stories, but without the. . .well, the inappropriate material.

- *Watch too much television.* If you're an avid television fan, you probably have a whole lineup of shows you enjoy. Dramas, reality shows, the Food Network. There's so much to choose from. But let's face it. . .some of us watch far too much television, and we often compromise our beliefs and morals to watch shows we know we shouldn't. (It's easy to get hooked, isn't it?) We allow television entertainment to fill our hours, stealing away time that could be better served. Here's a fun idea. If you want to join a Tuesday night Bible study but don't want to miss that favorite show, why not record it? That way you can zip through it in half the time later on. Ask the Lord how much television viewing is too much.

- *While away hours on the Internet.* It's easy to lose track of time when on the Internet. If you like to do things like researching your family lineage or sending encouraging e-mails to friends and family, that's one thing. And social networks (like Facebook and MySpace) can be a fun way to stay in touch with friends and family. But only in moderation. If you're frittering away your time, you might need a plan of action. Give yourself a specific window of time to spend online. "I'll spend an hour on the computer and no more." Why? Because the enemy would love nothing more than to steal your time. Why waste it on non-eternal things? Take a look at Rae's story:

It started pretty innocently. I would play games on the computer. Solitaire, mostly. Then TaiPei. Totally innocent stuff. They helped relax me after a long day at work. And, since I lived alone, there wasn't much to occupy my time once the dishes were done. But after awhile I noticed that I was staying up later and later. I got hooked on other games, some in online game rooms. It was fun, because I got to meet other people. But I noticed the time was getting away from me. Eleven o'clock turned into midnight. Midnight turned into one in the morning. Before long, I couldn't even go to sleep without my "game fix," and it was starting to affect me at work the following day. I finally set a time limit. A half hour. That was it. Now I'm at the point where I sometimes forget to get on the computer at all. I'm spending a lot more time taking care of housework and doing laundry, along with talking to my kids on the phone. Funny. I'd never even thought of it as a problem before.

- *Focus on yourself.* Does it surprise you to see that focusing on yourself (at least excessively) made it on the list? But some people do just that. If you're not careful, this empty-nest season can become a me-myself-and-I time. . . and that's never good. Whether you're focusing on your needs, your clothing, your appearance, your desires, your wants, your wishes. . .you need to keep it all in balance. Whenever you find most of your sentences starting with the word I, begin to shift your focus.

- *Drive your husband or children crazy with unnecessary attention.* Oh, that poor lonely empty-nest mom. She's accustomed to rushing in to save the day for everyone. Imagine the day when no one needs her. She reaches for the phone to give her son a call, hoping he has a problem she can solve. Or she sends several e-mails to her husband, just to let him know she's missing him. These things can be sweet. . .up to a point. Before you dial, pray. Call up the One who never gets tired of hearing from you. He will tell you what to do next. Savor that time with Him! It will prepare you for what comes next, whatever that may be.

- *Worry.* Some women are more prone to worry than others. They become skilled at it. If you're the type who can't sleep nights because you're worried about how your daughter is doing (in another state) or how your parents are doing

The House Is Quiet, *Now What?*

(perhaps due to health-related problems), then it's possible you're losing several hours a week fretting. A small amount of worry (or, rather, concern) is normal. But if you're giving up hours of your week to anxiety, you might want to visit with a counselor or your doctor. "Who of you by worrying can add a single hour to his life?" (Matthew 6:27 NIV).

- *Get into other people's business.* This is a tempting one if you've got a lot of free time on your hands. Maybe you get in the middle of a dispute between two friends or get caught up in a problem between your husband and his boss. Perhaps you get entangled in a dispute between your daughter and her boyfriend or two of your siblings. Regardless, it never pays off to take on a battle that is not your own, particularly if you cross the getting-into-other-people's-business line. Consider Brenda, whose life revolved around two things: her children and her work.

During a particularly busy season at the office I found myself in the middle of a dispute between two coworkers that threatened to bring more than a little disharmony to the office. At the same time, I also received multiple calls from my daughter who was having difficulty with a college roommate. One day with my daughter on the phone and my coworkers tossing barbs across the table in the break room, I knew I couldn't take it anymore. Before the end of the lunch hour, I'd not only phoned the troublesome roommate to solve the problem,

116

I also sat the coworkers down to fix their issues as well. Rather than return to my desk with harmony reigning, I found quite the opposite. Now they were all mad. At me. Certainly not the intended result, but definitely a danger if you go pole-vaulting over boundaries to handle things that are not yours to handle. I had to learn that the hard way!

What about you, Mom? Learn from Brenda's example and pray before you pick up that pole and go vaulting into a fray that's not yours. It might save not only your sanity but also your friendships. Not only that, with your time emptied of fretting over other people's concerns, you just might find you're able to enjoy your own life a whole lot more. Don't believe it? Try it and see!

It's possible to spend your free time on positive endeavors. And enjoy this season while you have it, Mom! Before long, someone is going to need you—a parent, a child, a husband, a friend, or even a pet!

◠ FLIGHT PATTERNS

Women respond differently to free time. Some loathe it because they feel lonesome. It reminds them of what they've lost. Others can't wait to get busy. They dive in headfirst! Let's look at a couple of stories to see how some empty-nest moms handle their free time. This first story is from Lyn:

> *I had the most wonderful feeling of release when our last one went off to college. We had successfully completed our years of following baseball and basketball schedules, band camps, youth camps, mission trips, and a houseful of teenagers. The first one's leaving was hard. I cried all the way home after dropping him off at college. The second one's exit was almost as hard, but by the time the youngest left, I was looking forward to having the house to ourselves and not having to pick up and clean up after the boys. Our youngest son did come back home to live from August until his wedding in January, but he had a job and career and was independent. He even contributed to our food bill. We have truly enjoyed the years since because we know they will come to visit with their families and chaos will reign for a few days, then peace and quiet will follow.*

Can you see how Lyn's perspective changed over time? She wept over the first child. . .celebrated over the last! Now let's see what Stephanie has to say:

After my four daughters married, I decided to go on a cruise with a good friend. We had a blast. However, I learned something about myself while basking on a private beach in Cozumel. I have a hard time being still. Being quiet. After years of chaos and fun, it's hard to still my mind and just. . .be. I found myself wanting to "do" something instead of just being there. (This probably came as a result of a works-based mentality. I'm a worker bee.) The Lord really began to convict me of this. After all, He'd given me this time—and this trip—as a gift. Why was I fretting over "being"? I'm now learning that part of the empty-nest experience is the ability to stop. Stop working. Stop fretting over kids. Stop thinking about the tasks ahead. . .and just be.

Some people are at a loss when it comes to free time. If you're one of those women who's never known how to relax, this is the perfect opportunity. Start by treating yourself to a massage or a pedicure. Then, take at least a few minutes out of each day to do something special for yourself.

We'll close with one more story, this one from Jacquie:

I've been an empty nester for almost ten years. I had a girl, then a boy seventeen months later. Life was so busy for me that I couldn't believe I would be facing a high-school graduation in 1998, then the next one in 1999. Back-to-back.

God is merciful in the process of "tapering off," though. The power struggles begin in middle school, so by the time they graduate from high school you're ready to see them move on into the real world and worrying about money. Ah-ha, sweet revenge! But it doesn't take long to miss those carpool lines, committee meetings, fund-raising campaigns, teacher conferences, ball games, choir programs, etc., because once they enter higher education, Mommy is no longer required to be a part.

Sounds like Jacquie had a pretty hectic schedule when the kids were growing up. (Can you imagine having children seventeen months apart?) Her hours were filled with the kids' to-do lists. Now that they're grown, she's free to make a to-do list of her own! And so are you, Mom. So, let's get to it!

◯ SMOOTH SAILING

Free time is just that: yours to do with as you will. Or, rather, as God says you should. Find good constructive ways to spend your free time. Before you pick up that questionable novel or hit the television remote, consider volunteering at a library or offering your services at a church ministry function.

Perhaps you're not one who has trouble filling those hours. Then you, dear sister, may need to monitor your time to be sure you're doing God's work in God's way and that you're not allowing your home life to suffer. Keep your boundaries firmly in place, love on your babies even though they are well past the baby stage. Walk the dog, feed the fish, or even better, pick up your Bible and spend some time with the One who created time itself. Remember your free time is precious and earned by all those hours spent raising the children who have flown from the nest. Enjoy!

- *The flowers appear on the earth; the time of the singing of birds is come, and the voice of the turtle is heard in our land.*
  SONG OF SOLOMON 2:12 KJV

- *By the seventh day God had finished the work he had been doing; so on the seventh day he rested from all his work.*
  GENESIS 2:2 NIV

- *"Come to me, all you who are weary and burdened, and I will give you rest."*
  MATTHEW 11:28 NIV

- *And my people shall dwell in a peaceable habitation, and in sure dwellings, and in quiet resting places.*
  ISAIAH 32:18 KJV

- *But make sure that you don't get so absorbed and exhausted in taking care of all your day-by-day obligations that you lose track of the time and doze off, oblivious to God. The night is about over, dawn is about to break. Be up and awake to what God is doing! God is putting the finishing touches on the salvation work he began when we first believed. We can't afford to waste a minute, must not squander these precious daylight hours in frivolity and indulgence, in sleeping around and dissipation, in bickering and grabbing everything in sight. Get out of bed and get dressed! Don't loiter and linger, waiting until the very last minute. Dress yourselves in Christ, and be up and about!*
  ROMANS 13:11–14 MSG

Chapter 6

WHEN THE NEST REFILLS

*Human beings are the only creatures on earth
that allow their children to come back home.*
BILL COSBY

◯ BYE-BYE, BIRDIE

Imagine this scenario. You've finally adapted to your new role as an empty nester. Your house is clean and the pungent scent of your son's tennis shoes is finally gone. You've reorganized, turning your daughter's bedroom into an office. You've satisfied your need for companionship by getting a dog, one who thinks you hung the moon. Your days are filled with work, church, friends, family, a blossoming marriage. . .and fun. Life is finally getting back to normal.

Then the unthinkable happens. Your son drops out of college and wants to come back home. . .for good. With his pit bull. Or maybe your married daughter and her husband go through a financial crisis and need a place to stay for a few months. . .with their six-month-old and a long-haired cat that makes you sneeze anytime you come within five feet of it. What do you do when those birdies fly back home, Mom? Are you open to the idea of refilling the nest, now that you've finally got it to yourself?

As you think about the way you might react to this news, ponder the New Testament story of Mary and Martha. As you probably remember, they had opposing viewpoints on how to do just about everything. One woman was more about relationship. The other was more about getting the job done and making sure the house was in perfect order. Perhaps there's a little of each in you. Your Mary side, full of tenderness and compassion, is longing to make things easier on your child, especially if he or she is in a jam. The Martha side is fretting over who's going to do the dishes, cook the meals, wash the clothes, mop the floor, and so forth. She may also be a little concerned about who's going to pay for everything. (Hey, someone's gotta foot the bill, right?)

Remember Gillian? She and her husband were enjoying a second honeymoon season when their son James—who had been on his own for four years—suddenly and through no fault of his own lost his job. He asked to move back home, and Gillian was torn. She loved her son, but she had also grown to love her privacy. Things were different this time around. Very different.

After much discussion, she and her husband reluctantly agreed that James could come back. Of course, he was a grown man now and would be expected to live more as a "roommate" than a child. While he was too old for a curfew, she did let him know about her schedule so that they could work out some ground rules to prevent potential conflicts. She gave up most of her office space, putting in a twin bed. At once, her grocery bill went up. Because her son was out of work, she "graced" him in this area. He wasn't in a position to help with the ever-growing utility bills, either.

At first, things went pretty well. Gillian loved the extra company. . .most of the time. Oh, she wasn't as keen on her son's friends and the amount of food they consumed. And over a period of time, she began to grow frustrated with the fact that James gave up on the job search in favor of sleeping late and playing video games until the wee hours of the morning. He didn't seem to mind mooching off Mom and Dad. But Gillian minded.

After a while, she and her husband opted to try a tough-love approach. They gave James a deadline to hit the job-hunting trail or risk losing his free room and board. They also put restrictions on the parts of his life that conflicted with theirs, namely the late nights and the numerous hungry friends. With the good nights' sleep he started getting and the lack of pals and video games to fill his empty hours, Gillian's son slowly but surely got his act together and found a job. A couple of months later, he moved back out and Gillian had her house—and her life—back. She breathed a huge sigh of relief, though she inwardly missed him after he left.

Have you walked a mile in Gillian's shoes? Have you had a grown child return home unexpectedly? Did you deal with financial or other issues related to this boomerang baby? The truth is, many parents (if not most) face this dilemma, and those who do allow the nest to refill can—and do—make good decisions for all involved. It just takes work. Sometimes *lots* of work!

So, what about you, Mama Bird? If and when those babies want to come back, what will you tell them? Have you given any thought to the fact that it might happen? It's best to have a plan of action, just in case. So, let's take a look at some of the challenges you might face. . .and some clever ways to handle them.

You see much more of your children once they leave home.
LUCILLE BALL

⟲ SPREADING YOUR WINGS

Let's face it. . .living with people is tough, especially when those people are no longer docile and obedient children, but rather opinionated and strong-willed adults. Every person in a household has his or her own way of doing things. Some are sloppy. Others are picky. Some are night owls. Some are early birds. Some like junk food; others wouldn't touch the stuff. When you merge differing thoughts and ideas, there's bound to be controversy! This can be even more exaggerated when a grown child comes home. When that happens, you have to factor in additional issues, like, "Am I going to be taken advantage of?" or even, "Will this destroy our relationship?"

Let's take a look at some of the issues you might be facing if Johnny comes marching home again:

- Whose house is it, anyway? (A legitimate question!)

- Who's bailing out whom? (And will this lead to resentment?)

- How many housemates can I handle? (People, people, and more people!)

- What's the plan? (You've gotta have one!)

- Who pays? (Groceries, utilities, rent, etc.)

- Who does what? (Cleaning, cooking, childcare, etc.)

- Whose schedule? (Yours, mine, or ours?)

- Where will it all go? (Oy, that stuff!)

- Rearrange—again? (Just when I finally got things where I want them!)

- Will my beliefs be compromised? (Differences in belief)

- What about pet issues? (Here, Fido!)

- What does R.E.S.P.E.C.T. mean?

- Has the dress code been "covered"?

- Gratitude or resentment? (Will this lead to bitterness or resentment?)

- Can't we all just get along? (Ah, the ultimate question!)

As you can see, there is a lot to consider when you think about having a grown child back in your home. And this can be even more complicated if it's the other way around (you move in with a grown child). Still, it is possible to work things out in such a way that everyone is satisfied and happy. Sure, you'll have your ups and downs, but ultimately, you really can make it work. . .with the Lord's help.

◯ LIFTOFF!

So, you've made your decision and you're sticking with it. You're about to merge lives—and homes—with an adult child. Whether they're moving in with you or you're moving in with them, there are still issues to be worked out. Let's go over that list one more time, this time focusing on some solutions.

- *Whose house is it, anyway?* You might wonder why we're starting with this issue. It is the very one that the enemy can and will use to drive a wedge between you and your loved ones, if you let him. Of course, there are two scenarios, and each has to be handled differently. Let's say your grown son is moving into your home. It is still your home, but you want him to feel comfortable and welcome. This means you have to have a shift in attitude. If you're willingly opening your heart and home to him, you can't continually rub it in that it's "your" home. You're one big happy family now. And you should expect the same if you're moving in with your child. They should make you feel welcome. That said, it's important to understand that the person with longevity in the home will always feel the stronger sense of ownership and should have the final say, at least in many cases. And, of course, there are financial issues that drive the point home even more. If you're paying the mortgage or rent, for instance, your feelings of possessiveness will be much stronger. This is fine, but be careful not to rub things in.

- *Who's bailing out whom?* Imagine this scenario. You're a single mom with grown kids. You go through a health crisis and (doctor's orders!) can't live alone. You move in with your married son and his wife. (Can you sense trouble already?) In a sense, they are bailing you out. However, the goal here is to never make anyone feel like they're not welcome, especially if the circumstance is beyond his or her control. Now imagine the opposite scenario. Your grown daughter separates from her husband and needs a place to stay for a while with her two-year-old daughter. It's not her fault, but living together causes a few rifts. You occasionally feel the need to point the finger. Here's your goal. . .don't shame or blame if the other person has no control over his or her circumstances. On the other hand, if you're dealing with irresponsibility, understand that there's a line between helping and enabling. You have to decide which one of those you're doing, especially if your grown child moves into your place and brings some nasty habits with him or her.

- *How many housemates can I handle?* If you've grown accustomed to living in a quiet, peaceful house, you'll surely run into a problem when the house refills. This will be complicated further if your son or daughter brings home a spouse or children. Let's take a look at Geena's story:

    How about thinking you're an empty nester, then having a burst of grandchildren you nanny for? I have friends whose children were grown and left home, then, because their son-in-law ended up in jail, they've been raising their three young grandchildren.

Are you psychologically prepared, Mom. . .even for the most unheard of circumstances? If not, you'd better rethink your plan. Because once those people are in your home, they will sense any resentment. If you do decide to move forward, continually seek the Lord for how He wants you to treat your new housemates. It's going to take some work, but if you ask for His input in each individual circumstance, He will give it. Here's one final thought about the influx of people. . .sometimes your son or daughter will move back in and invite his or her friends to hang out. If it looks like they're taking over your space, you'll need to talk it through.

- *What's the plan?* If you're going to merge lives, you need a clear plan. You've got to know the answer to most of the questions that could crop up before they come up. Is that possible? Yes. With a plan. Before your grown child moves in, make a list of specific things. How much rent will be paid by each party (if applicable)? Who gets which room? Who controls which television? Who will do the laundry? Who will purchase the groceries? Schedule issues. Pet issues. Don't leave anything out! If you're clear about who does what ahead of time, you can't point fingers after the fact. Unless someone deviates from the plan, that is. Even then, extend grace and mercy as much as you are able. Sure, living with your grown child is different from before. That's why you must have a long discussion before you ever agree to it. There have to be ground rules so everyone is clear. Write everything down so no one can dispute the finer points. If there's ever a dispute, the final decision should probably rest with the homeowner. That person needs to be taking the lead, making sure she's comfortable. The other person asks. The homeowner gives permission. The reverse of that is, once you say yes, you can't get bitter. You've got to have a we're-going-to-make-this-work attitude throughout!

- *Who pays?* This is a tricky one only if you haven't created a plan ahead of time. If your grown child has a job, it's always a good idea to charge rent, even if it's just a token amount. The same holds true for grocery and utility bills. You'll have to discuss all of this in advance, of course, and it's going to vary, depending on each party's financial issues and the specific situation. There are times when you deliberately go out of your way to help the other person through a hard time. Consider Annie's story:

When my daughter was seven months pregnant with her third daughter, her husband was laid off from his job. They lost their home to foreclosure and had no other place to go, so I took them in. Having two feisty little girls around (as well as two grownups) was quite a switch from my quiet, peaceful life. However, I loved the company. For a while. It took my son-in-law months to find a job, and there were many months when I had to cover the cost of the food, utilities, and so on. My daughter faced some unexpected complications with her pregnancy and was hospitalized for a week. Their finances took a further downturn during that time and I actually helped them out with all of that, too. I did my best not to rub this in. I knew their situation was dire (and we're talking about my daughter's health here). Once my son-in-law found a job, I helped them get into a new house (paying their deposit and first month's rent). Was this the right move? For me, yes. I knew the time was right but I also knew it would take a couple of months for them to get on their feet. Having them with me cost me financially, but I actually enjoyed that season of my life.

- *Who does what?* More people means more work. And with more work comes the all-important question: who does what? To be more specific, who cooks? Who cleans? Who takes care of yard work? This is now a team effort, but the list of responsibilities needs to be clearly laid out ahead of time. Bitterness can grow if you're not clear on which person handles which chore. Here are a couple of ideas to ease the pain in this area: Take turns. Make a rotating schedule for cooking, cleaning, etc. Or, if you're not comfortable with that plan, take a close look at how and where the various people excel. Are you the best cook? Do you love preparing meals for others? Maybe you should take on that role. Is your son or son-in-law able to handle the yard work? Awesome! Is your daughter a cleaning fanatic? Maybe she's the one to handle most of the cleaning. You might have to try out different scenarios to see which works best, but you will work it out!

- *Whose schedule?* Different people. . .different schedules. Some are problematic; others are not. Here's the key. . . everyone involved has to agree to be considerate. If you're one of those "early to bed, early to rise" people and your son or daughter is a night owl, you'll have to lay some ground rules. No loud music late at night. Guests need to go home by a certain time. Same holds true in the mornings. If you're up early, you might need to be extra quiet as you make your breakfast, especially if there are sleeping babies involved. You'll get adjusted to things over time and won't even notice them anymore. The key is to talk about what your needs are ahead of time. Compare notes. And as for the age-old question, do I set a curfew for my grown child?. . .well, good luck with that. It's probably better not to, as long as he or she agrees to tiptoe in, or call you if he or she is going to stay overnight someplace else. Otherwise, you'll be up all night worrying!

- *Where will it all go?* Sometimes kids leave home but don't take all their things with them. Other times they return and bring not only what they took but also tons of other stuff. In either case, the question must be asked: where will it all go? Sometimes there's enough room in the attic or garage to accommodate the dual household items. Decide now, Mama Bird, whether you're willing to give up your garage space for your child's furniture. Perhaps you're fine with it, or maybe you aren't. Either way, it is important that you have a plan ahead of time to avoid the issue of stacking the second set of dining room chairs in the corner of the room and being forced to surround yourself with moving boxes. Perhaps a storage unit is in order. Great! But be sure and decide who is paying for it and what will go in it. Two households can combine, but only if there's a plan in place for easing the transition.

• *Rearrange—again?* It's enough to break your heart! You've just got your house like you want it. Then, suddenly, you've got a houseful. Son. Daughter-in-law. Two kids. You give up your office space, moving the computer into the kitchen. The bookshelves? Well, you somehow squeeze those into your living room, which now has a kiddie table and chairs along with your original furniture. You give up the guest room, telling your parents they'll have to stay on the sleeper sofa if they come for a visit. And then there's the issue of the garage. It's packed from floor to ceiling, not just with your stuff, but your kids', as well. The pantry is loaded with food from two different cupboards. And the pots and pans? They're everywhere! Whose stuff do you use? And what do you do with the leftovers? There's really only one way to make this part work, Mom. You've got to be completely and totally organized. . .and you've got to stay that way once the crowd arrives. Take a look at Hillary's story:

> *I'd just moved into my new home—completely alone, I might add—when my daughter approached me about*

moving in and I agreed. (She and her little girl had been living in another city and I was thrilled to have them!) Only one problem. . .the stuff! I had a houseful of furniture already, and I'd just set it up like I wanted it! However, I quickly made up my mind that we would make this work. So, we began to shuffle things around. Before long, the house contained more furniture than should be allowed by law. But we managed all right. The garage was loaded (I couldn't park my car inside anymore), but we found a way to get the important stuff inside. Only one problem remained. . .every time I opened the pantry, spices fell out! We had an overabundance of them!

- *Will my beliefs be compromised?* Sometimes parents and their grown kids have completely different beliefs, not just about who and how they worship, but about life in general. And when you're living together, that can get sticky. Take a look at Pam's story:

When my grown daughter and I got an apartment together just after my divorce, I made up my mind: stick to your morals. For me this meant no overnight guests of the opposite sex and no smoking in the house. One time she threw a party and served alcohol, but hardly anyone showed up. I expected respect from anyone who visited. One time she asked if her boyfriend could move in. I was so shocked that she would dare to ask! She called me at work to ask and I told her I would have to get back to her, that this was not something I could discuss on the phone from work. In my car I cried out and fussed at the Lord about it. A few days passed, then I went into her room and told her that I could not set aside my convictions and allow him to live with her in our home. She ended up moving out and in with him at his parents'. They eventually got an apartment together, had a child, then got married. The marriage did not last. Sometimes, if your grown children share rent and expenses, it is more difficult to place restrictions. . . . You have to deal with situations as they arise. But I think things can be discussed, and let the fault be yours that you cannot go against your convictions. You don't judge them but you can judge yourself and know what the Lord expects of you.

• *What about pet issues?* If you're a pet lover but your grown child is not (or vice versa), you might have a few issues to work out. And those issues can be complicated if someone happens to be allergic to little Fifi, or if your daughter's cat shreds the arms of your sofa with her claws. And even if you're crazy about dogs, cats, rabbits, mice, etc., living with them isn't always easy, especially if some of those little critters aren't house-trained. The whole family needs to work together on this one, Mom. You've got to have a common goal. Why? Because animals are fickle. They need consistent, strategic training. Don't let your love (or disdain) for a pet ruin your relationship with a child. It's not worth it.

- *What does R.E.S.P.E.C.T. mean?* What does it take to make you feel respected? And how do you treat others with respect? Part of this has to do with picking your battles. Some of it is about setting boundaries. (Not going into someone's room unannounced, no blaring music or video games late at night, etc.) If you have a married couple in your house, don't interrupt their bedroom space. If your babies have moved in with babies of their own, balance your critique with your care. By the same token, you should be treated respectfully as well. This means your grown child has to watch how she talks to you and how she treats your home (if, indeed, she is living in your home and not the other way around). Take a look at Maria's story.

> *I've been a single mom most of my adult life. My three kids rarely saw their dad. When my youngest son (who was forty-four at the time) asked if he could move back home after his divorce, I reluctantly agreed. I didn't realize until he arrived that he'd developed a taste for alcohol. Then I started seeing evidence of Internet pornography. I confronted him, but he refused to change his ways, stating, "I'm not a kid anymore. Stop treating me like one." Before long, the beer bottles were filling my house, and my personal computer was loaded with images I couldn't bear to see. He refused to treat me with the respect I deserved, so I eventually had to ask him to move out. It took some convincing, but he finally got his own place. He has since cleaned up his act and has even*

139

remarried. Still, the decision to ask him to leave was the right one. I honestly think it saved our relationship.

- *Has the dress code been "covered"?* This is a tricky one for women who've never lived with a son. Let's say your grown daughter and her husband move in for a few months while they're waiting for a house to be built. You're used to getting up in the morning, padding into the kitchen in your nightie, and fixing breakfast. You try it the first morning, only to realize your son-in-law is standing in the kitchen in his tighty-whities, drinking a cup of coffee. It's time to implement a new dress code. . .and quick! Sure, it means changing habits, and it might even mean losing that relaxed-in-my-own-home feeling. But this season will pass, and before long you can wear what you want when you want!

- *Gratitude or resentment?* It's so important that you make up your mind at the onset not to let bitterness or resentment grow. If you're the one on the receiving end (you're moving in with a grown child because you have no choice), maintain an attitude of gratitude. If it's the other way around (especially if your child has no control over his or her circumstances), be careful not to shame or blame. And guard passive-aggressive reactions. These are those "subliminal" messages that leak through when you didn't really want the living arrangement in the first place but said yes anyway. These reactions can often arise when the other person isn't carrying through with his or her end of the bargain. Honesty is always the best policy. And when the times come to speak the truth. . .do it in love.

- *Can't we all just get along?* Despite the fact you gave birth to this child and raised him or her until the nest emptied, you're now faced with a relationship that has been altered a bit. Embrace the change but don't allow the child to rule the roost—unless the coop's not yours. Set limits, make a plan, and give God first place in all of it. These things can work, dear one, but only if you factor the Lord in first.

In spite of your best attempts, there will be times when you will feel like your home isn't yours. With your decision to take on new housemates comes a price: sanity and having the house to yourself.

Here's a great way to remedy any angst you might be feeling, Mom. Create a spot in the house that's still yours. Your room. A quiet place. A back porch or deck. You have to get it set in your mind that you can still retreat to that spot. Be comfortable. Have a Bible nearby. A place to sit with your coffee cup. Make a little nest to yourself when the big nest is full. It may need to be communicated to the group that your spot is your spot. Period.

If you need to, have the good sense to go someplace. Head to Starbucks. Drive to the park. Take photos of birds. Do something that relaxes you. When you need this time, go alone. Don't take a grandchild with you. You'll be surprised what a little "alone" time will do, especially if you're really hoping to work things out. Deep breath, Mama Bird! This nest might be full, but with God at the center, you really can live happily ever after with the now-grown chicks inside.

> *There isn't a child who hasn't gone out into the*
> *brave new world who eventually doesn't return to the*
> *old homestead carrying a bundle of dirty clothes.*
> ART BUCHWALD

◌ FLIGHT PATTERNS

While there are a host of families moving back in together, every situation is different. Different dynamics. Different financial obligations. Different workloads. Because there are so many different scenarios, we've included four brief stories of empty-nest moms who triumphed over their challenges when the kids moved back in. Let's start with Becky's story:

> *I must confess, I was a little selfish with my space when my daughter and her husband moved in. I wasn't always gracious and even rubbed things in a time or two. I had to do business with the Lord about this because my son-in-law had cancer and my daughter was doing her best to work and care for him. After much prayer on the matter, I changed my thinking. I developed a can-do attitude. My son-in-law is now in remission and the happy couple has moved on. I honestly miss them!*

Now let's look at Hannah's story:

I was an empty nester until my son moved back home to go to our local college instead of the big university he attended last year. Prior to that, both kids had been gone and since hubby works second shift, it was just me and the dog. I'm loving having my son back home—probably one of those parents who don't know when to stop mothering.

Now take a look at Marian's views on the matter. She's one of those consummate moms who loves having a full house!

I was an empty nester, then the birdies flew back to the nest. I hated it while they were away. The house didn't have the same rhythm to it.

Maybe you're like that, too, Mom. Maybe you enjoy having a full house. Some women do!

Finally, let's sneak a peek at what Tracie had to say:

Empty nest? What's that? Now if we were talking about adult "tenants," well then I would have plenty to say on the subject!

Does that bring a smile to your face? Sounds like she knows what she's talking about, doesn't it?

Things that once seemed negative can easily be turned positive, including that surprise refilling of the nest. Are you a Hannah or a Tracie? Perhaps you're a Becky or a Marian. Whichever you are, there's only one thing to be: grateful. Yes, grateful! Nothing lasts forever, including this. Soon you'll be seeing a not-so-full nest again. It's just a matter of time. . .and prayer!

C SMOOTH SAILING

Funny how sometimes that thing you pray for—the nest filling once again—can be the very prayer that gets answered well after you expect it to. Take heart, Mama Bird, when the young ones return to the nest. Before feathers can fly, make a plan and stick to it. This really is survivable, but only with the Lord guiding your steps.

See what the Lord has to say about seeking Him in all things, including navigating the perplexing flight plan that is the returning of now-grown chicks to the nest.

- *Then Jehoshaphat said, "But before you do anything, ask GOD for guidance."*
  2 CHRONICLES 18:4 MSG

- *"For I know the plans I have for you," says the LORD. "They are plans for good and not for disaster, to give you a future and a hope."*
  JEREMIAH 29:11 NLT

- *He must manage his own family well, having children who respect and obey him.*
  1 TIMOTHY 3:4 NLT

- *Blessed is the man who perseveres under trial, because when he has stood the test, he will receive the crown of life that God has promised to those who love him.*
  JAMES 1:12 NIV

- *"So there is hope for your future," declares the LORD. "Your children will return to their own land."*
  JEREMIAH 31:17 NIV

Chapter 7

THE SANDWICH GENERATION

First we are children to our parents, then parents to our children,
then parents to our parents, then children to our children.
MILTON GREENBLAT

C BYE-BYE, BIRDIE

Life is filled with interesting twists and turns. Here's one that often catches empty nesters by surprise. Say your children are all grown and you've grown accustomed to your life in this new role. Then one or both of your parents become incapacitated, unable to live alone, and you take on the role of caregiver. You're once again in the saddle, caring for someone, but this time you don't know the rules of the game. How do you parent a parent? Are you called to do that, or have you misunderstood the rules? Many empty nesters face this very thing, and feel lost as a result.

And then there's the opposite scenario. You finally have time to devote to your aging parents, but you can't find them! They're off in the RV, traveling the country and spending your inheritance. Their motto? "Well, we can't take it with us!" You'd like to invite them to your son's wedding, but they're off gallivanting and can't be bothered. Now what?

If your children are grown and your parents (or in-laws) are still alive, then you are officially part of what is known as "the sandwich generation." Take a look at this quote from Sheri and Bob Stritof, authors of "The Cluttered Nest Syndrome."

What is the Sandwich Generation? It is a demanding time when a couple is still dealing with parenting issues, thinking about their own retirement, and yet facing the issues of coping with aging parents. Deciding which has the highest priority can tear a marriage apart. An estimated 22 percent of the American population can be classified as the Sandwich Generation, meaning they are parenting

*their own children and taking care of their parents at the
same time. Some estimates show that nearly two-thirds of
the baby boom generation will be taking care of an elderly
parent in the next ten years. In 1990,* Newsweek *reported
that the average woman spends 17 years raising children
and 18 years helping aging parents.* [6]

As a member of the sandwich generation, you face divided
loyalties. You're split down the middle between caring for your
children and your parents. And what a tug of war! While neither
group is particularly demanding at times, life can often throw
curve balls. Say your daughter is going through a divorce at the
same time your mother is diagnosed with breast cancer. Now
what? Whose needs do you tend to first? You are sandwiched
between the two and your once-freed-up schedule is now filled
to the max. You're back to the point where you're giving out. . .
to everyone but yourself. But what choice do you have?

Remember Gillian? She faced a rough road about three years
into her empty-nest life. Her father suddenly and unexpectedly
passed away, leaving Gillian's mother alone in a nearby city. At
about this same time, Gillian's daughter started experiencing
problems with her pregnancy. Gillian ran herself ragged, going
back and forth between the two. At times, she couldn't figure
out who had the greater need, her mother or her daughter. She
wrestled with guilt, never feeling like she was giving either the
right amount of time and attention. Thankfully, her daughter
gave birth to a beautiful baby girl in due time with no further

---

[6] Sheri and Bob Stritof, "The Cluttered Nest Syndrome," http://marriage.about.
com/cs/sandwich/a/sandwichgen.htm. (Used with permission.)

complications. Gillian was finally able to catch her breath, though she now had a grandbaby to factor into the mix! Ironically, Gillian's mom remarried two years later, so life shifted gears once again.

Have you walked a mile in Gillian's shoes? Do you know what it's like to care for parent and child simultaneously? Has life ever shifted. . .then shifted again? Here's the deal, Mom. 'Tis the season. It's your age and your stage. And you are certainly not the first to find yourself caught between parent and child. The sandwich generation has always existed. Your mom went through it, likely. And your grandmother.

Here's the truth, Mom. As long as there have been people on planet Earth, there's been a sandwich generation. Only our attitudes have changed, not our situations. Folks in biblical times lived much differently than we do. In those days, the elderly parents were a part of the household, cared for by the children. Only in the past fifty years has that changed. But don't fret it. . .and don't sweat it! This isn't something you need to dread. There's something about this season that strengthens you for the road ahead. You'll face losses and gains, joys and sorrows. But God will walk you through them all. "For nothing will be impossible with God" (Luke 1:37 NASB).

If you're caught in the middle between your aging parents and your grown children, step back. Take a deep breath. Ask the Lord what He desires for you to do. Perhaps He's not calling you to rush in and rescue anyone. Or maybe He's got a plan that makes far more sense than what you're considering now. Either way, the stresses of this season don't have to throw you for a loop. Take slow, calculated steps. Set clearly defined plans in motion. And don't get ahead of God. He will lead you all the way.

◠ SPREADING YOUR WINGS

If you're a member of the sandwich generation, you're caught in three worlds at once. . .the world of your children and the world of your parents. And then there's your own world. Remember all of those things you wanted to do with your spare time? Renovate your master bathroom? Teach a Bible study? Join a health club? How can you possibly do all of that and still have time left over for people who genuinely need you?

So, you're stuck in the middle and encountering some situations you never expected. In order to deal with those issues, you've got to face them. See them for what they are. Let's take a look at some of the things sandwich-generation women may face:

- Bona fide needs (of a parent or a child)
- The needy mother or father
- The needy child
- Abandonment by parents
- Abandonment by child
- Caretaking issues
- The fix-it mentality

- Resentment

- Financial issues

- Long-term planning

- Loss of traditions

- Lack of emotional ties

- Feelings of guilt

- Feelings of loss

◯ LIFTOFF!

If you stand a chance of getting through this season, you need a plan. A strategy. It's time to take a look at those issues once again, this time with a creative eye. For every potential problem there is an effective solution.

- *Bona fide needs.* When it comes to aging parents, there are some very real needs to be addressed. Do they have the funds they need to make it through this season of life? Have they set a plan in motion as to where they will spend their retirement years? Are they independent, or will they require hands-on care? Are they reluctant to share their needs with you? Do they have long-term insurance? Is housing an issue? Do they need help with estate planning? And what about your kids? They have bona fide issues, too. Your daughter has decided to switch her major and needs your input. Your son is getting married and you need to help him plan a rehearsal dinner. Your daughter-in-law is giving birth to twins and wants your help. "Calgon, take me away!" becomes your battle cry! Slow, steady breaths, Mom. One thing at a time. One person at a time. One calamity at a time. Stop right now, right here, and decide. . .you will not take a step in anyone's direction (though the needs are great) without checking in with the Lord first. He will guide you through. . .one person, one situation, at a time. Take a look at Susan's story:

I still remember that summer like it was yesterday. We'd been helping my son plan his wedding for months. How were we supposed to know my father would get sick that very week? And my mother? Dad ended up in one hospital on the east side of town and Mom in a hospital on the west side. The wedding, thank goodness, was smack-dab between them. I ping-ponged from place to place to place as we made arrangements with the facility and cared for my parents. Sadly, neither were able to attend the wedding, but, in the end, they both recovered and the big day came off without a hitch. (That was truly a miracle, all things considered!)

- *The needy mother or father.* You love your parents and want to be there for them as much as you are able. But lately, things have been difficult. One or the other of them is constantly calling. You're expected to stop everything you're doing and run to the rescue. It is often difficult to tell if a need is genuine or if a person is just acting needy because he or she is lonely or feeling a little selfish. This is often a real struggle as you deal with aging parents. Some of them have legitimate needs—health, financial, stress, grieving, loneliness, and so on. Others are demanding and require constant input from their children. Some of these in the latter category have turned manipulation into an art form! When looking at the situation with your parents, start with this question: am I being manipulated or is there a real need here? If the need is real (and it often is), then talk with your spouse (if you have one; a friend, otherwise) and be sure to consult the Lord. Come up with a plan. But if the need is not real, then you might have to learn to implement a little tough love. Take a look at Gloria's story:

When my mother turned seventy, her approach to life changed. She'd always been bright and cheerful, but she turned sour after my dad died. I knew loneliness was at the core of it and did my best to spend significant time with her and treat her kindly, even when she snapped at me. But she didn't always make it easy. She called a lot, demanding attention and constantly accusing us of not doing enough for her. I knew her accusations weren't legitimate. We'd bent over backwards to meet her financial and emotional needs already and always included her in family events. It really came down to one word: attention. She would get it. . .one way or the other. It reminded me of my son when he was in middle

*school. . .acting out to get attention from the teacher and/
or peers. Though it was the hardest thing I've ever done,
I finally had to sit down with my mom and address this
issue in a "tough love" sort of way. She cried, which broke
my heart. But in the end, she confessed that she was
really dealing with loneliness and just needed to hear my
voice (on the phone or in person). I call her several times
a week now. In fact, I'm usually the one to initiate our
conversations. I also take her to lunch every Wednesday
at a local tearoom, which she loves. She has since joined
a dance class at the YMCA and is dating a new beau! Go
figure!*

- *The needy child.* And then there's the needy child. Oh, you
know the one. He's always been sort of a mama's boy and
needs your input for every little thing. He's physically out
of the nest, but you sometimes wonder if he'll ever make
the leap emotionally. You get caught up in his financial
dealings, his relationship problems, his poor study habits
at college, his angst with his girlfriend, and even his
floundering spiritual life. In short, you're in over your
head and you're drowning. Still, he's your boy and you
don't know how to stop the codependent cycle. What's a
poor mom to do? Take a giant step back. Your needy child
will continue to be needy as long as you let him. He's not
going to stop on his own, so you must stop the madness
yourself. Draw a line in the sand. Make up your mind.
"This far and no farther." Help him as much as the Lord
allows, but don't overstep your bounds. If you do, you'll be

taking on the role of God in his life. And there's only place for one leader!

- *Abandonment by parents.* Maybe you're concerned about your parents because they don't seem to stay in touch. Some empty nesters go through this. They long for a deeper relationship with a mother or father, but they can't seem to slow down either parent long enough to see it come to pass. Check out Kendra's story:

  When I was a kid, my parents spent every spare dollar on my brother and me. Ballet lessons. Piano lessons. Sports. You name it, we had it. To compensate financially, we didn't take a lot of elaborate vacations. A few road trips, but nothing grand. Now that my brother and I are grown, we can't find my parents! We never know where they are. Last year they flew off to London for a week, but didn't tell us until they got there! A few months after that, they bought an RV and we've hardly seen them since. It's weird. I always thought of my mom and dad as being such homebodies, but it turned out they were only that way for a season. Sometimes I want to invite my parents over for dinner, but they're busy. With their friends. Their church group. Their RV club. I've reconciled myself to the fact that my mom and dad are now world travelers. Maybe one day I will be, too.

- *Abandonment by child.* This is a tough one, especially if you're sensitive. Imagine this scenario. You haven't seen your daughter in months because she's been attending a college on the other side of the country. You're funding her entire existence, but it's worth it. Then Christmas arrives and you're thrilled! You make all sorts of plans, knowing she will jump in with both feet. Unfortunately, she only breezes in and out of your house long enough to say "hello" and "good-bye." She's far more interested in catching up with her friends and high-school classmates. Can't imagine something like this happening? It does. Every day. Empty-nest moms get their hopes up, then find those hopes dashed. There's only one way to deal with feelings of abandonment. You have to give them to the Lord. He alone knows how to replace them with wholeness. Your child will disappoint you. No doubt about that. But God never will.

- *Caretaking issues.* Perhaps you've become a full-time caregiver for one of your parents. If this is the case, don't try to carry the whole load. Get other people—doctors, neighbors, pastors, church friends—involved. This is how Wendy handled this situation:

> *My mom was widowed at an early age and always got along pretty well on her own until her heart attack. After that, I found myself going back and forth to her house nearly every day. My brother (the only other sibling) lived in another town. And my husband (God bless him) helped, too. My mom recovered to the point where she could get around and get back to living, but I still fretted*

over the fact that she spent the nights alone in her house. So, I contacted one of her neighbors and we implemented a plan of action. If my mom's porch light was still on after nine o'clock at night—or if the newspaper hadn't been picked up the next morning—the neighbor would report in. I also contacted my mom's pastor and made sure folks from the church would drop in on her occasionally. Some even brought meals when she wasn't feeling well. I found that sharing the load really helped.

- *The fix-it mentality.* Are you a fixer? One of those people who tend to sweep in and take the reins? Then it's likely you're going to be very busy! "Fixers" rush to the rescue when someone is in need. And let's face it. . .you're probably seeing a lot of needs with both your parents and your kids right now. Before you jump into action, ask God (the ultimate Fixer) for His opinion. He may use you at times to fix problems for others. But it's just as likely He wants to take care of things another way.

- *Resentment.* Perhaps you looked forward to this time in your life, even made plans to do all those things you put off while raising kids. And now, contrary to what you expected, you're not on the road, seeing America through an RV windshield. Instead, you're looking at the world through your mother's nursing home window. Or perhaps it's a hospital room. Or maybe you're still standing in your driveway because your garage is filled with those things your daughter, son, mother, or father brought along when he or she moved in. Now all you want to do is fume—or cry—when you think of the glorious plans that have gone horribly awry. Take heart, sandwiched sister. The Lord may have allowed your circumstances to be rearranged, but He will also walk you through this. Refuse to let this altered situation steal your joy. Instead, thank Him for giving you the strength for this hour, for this minute. The rest will happen as God ordains, and you won't have wasted time fretting and complaining in the interim.

- *Financial issues.* Oy, the money! Where does it go? College tuition for your youngest son. Helping your mom with her utilities because her social security check doesn't quite cover her costs. Rushing to your oldest son's rescue when his car needs repair. Paying for your daughter's wedding. Purchasing medicines or supplies for your aging parents. And, just about the time you think you can't handle any more, you discover your parents haven't been setting aside adequate monies for their retirement years. They need your help coming up with a plan of action. How can you handle it all? As you think about these many things, take a look at Carlee's story:

My parents were always pretty tight-lipped about their finances, so I never really knew what sort of shape they were in financially. I assumed they were doing okay because they never did without and they traveled quite a bit. It was only after my father's death that I found out they were mortgaged to the hilt. And my mom's propensity

*for shopping didn't help! My husband and I swept in,
loaning her money and paying off some of the debt. Before
long, however, creditors were calling once again. At about
this same time, our college-aged son was in an accident
and was hospitalized for two and a half months. It was
a long and expensive process, one that insurance covered
only in part. We found ourselves strapped, trying to
cover everything. I finally had to sit down with my mom
and work out a budget (which she still struggles with).
Fortunately, a secondary automobile policy paid the
balance on my son's hospitalization. Still, it was a rough
season!*

- *Long-term planning.* A lot of us in the sandwich
  generation don't think about helping our parents out
  with long-term planning, but it's likely they need
  our input. Have they made provision for where they
  will spend their golden years? Are their investments
  secure? Do they have proper medical coverage (beyond
  Medicare)? Are they vulnerable to identity theft? Have
  they taken care of estate planning? Is there a will in
  place? Do they have an attorney? If so, do you know
  how to reach him or her? These are all things you should
  sit down and discuss with your parents. After taking a
  look at Claire's story below, you'll see why:

  *I didn't think it was possible for my dad to be "taken
  in" by anyone because he's such a bright man. But the
  same year he started showing signs of dementia, he*

was swindled! It was one of those Internet scams where someone asked for his banking information. He fell right into the swindler's hands, giving out all of his personal information. Before long, the bank account was empty and the thief had hightailed it across the country. We never caught the person, but it still chaps me every time I think of it. As you can imagine, I've since had a long conversation with both of my parents, pointing out the dangers of identity theft. Sadly, my father's condition has deteriorated to the point where I've been put in charge of his finances, anyway. (What is left of them. The thief wasn't able to get into my parents' retirement account, thank goodness.)

- *Loss of traditions.* Empty nesters (even those whose parents have already passed away) often face an interruption of family traditions. Thanksgiving dinner. Christmas presents under the tree. Easter service at church. Everything you've done routinely for years now stands threatened. In fact, you wonder if any of your traditions will survive! Take a look at Megan's story:

  Man, what a mess! I'm part of that empty nest/ sandwich generation and it wreaks havoc on family traditions. We used to get everyone together on Christmas Day—my parents, my kids, and us. Now planning for holidays is a nightmare! My daughter has a new family to consider now. So does my son. My mom passed away last year and I like to keep my dad in the loop, but he's been pretty withdrawn lately. Says he doesn't like the holidays because they make him miss Mom. I understand that, but I feel like our old traditions are slipping away. Finally, in desperation, I came up with a new plan. If we couldn't do "traditional" holidays, we'd do untraditional ones. I changed the dates. Changed the menus. Changed everything. Now we do a huge family get-together every couple of months. We call it the Kenner Clan meeting. Most often we'll barbecue or have a picnic in a local park where the grandkids can play. That way, we're starting a whole new tradition.

- *Lack of emotional ties.* Those in the sandwich generation can feel like they're losing relationships in both directions. Instead of struggling with fears about this, resolve yourself to strengthening those ties by sending cards, letters, and so forth. Don't worry if your child or parent doesn't reciprocate. Don't get your feelings hurt. Continue to reach out (though not in an obsessive way), even when you're not receiving anything in response. Your kids are going through a season where they're just not as tied to you as they once were. But they will be. As soon as they get married, start having babies, etc., they'll be back. And those emotional ties will be stronger than ever.

- *Feelings of guilt.* Some in the sandwich generation feel like they're so torn that they can't do anything right. Maybe you can relate. You want to go to your mom's choir presentation at her church, but your granddaughter is singing at a different church on the same day. You would love to go to lunch with your dad, but your son is leaving to go back to college tomorrow and this is your last day with him. Sometimes it's overwhelming, especially if people go overboard in their reactions. Even if a parent or child is disappointed, you don't have to feel guilty. You're doing the best you can do. Decide here and now not to give guilt or condemnation a foothold. You will never be able to meet everyone's needs. Nor should you have to. "There is therefore now no condemnation to them which are in Christ Jesus, who walk not after the flesh, but after the Spirit" (ROMANS 8:1 KJV).

- *Feelings of loss.* It's natural for an empty nester to go through feelings of loss. You face them when your kids leave for school, when they marry, or when they move away to another city or state. You also face feelings of loss as your parents age, though those feelings are a bit harder to define. Some in the empty-nest generation are inundated with feelings of impending loss, especially if they're walking a parent through an illness. It's so important that you not let fear rob you of the time you have together. Relax. Breathe deeply. Enjoy the moments! Instead of dreading impending losses, be thankful for the promise of today.

Whew! That's a lot to think about, isn't it? When you're sandwiched between parents and kids, you're bound to stay plenty busy. But don't forget to take care of yourself along the way. After all, you're no good to others unless you're in good shape yourself!

◯ FLIGHT PATTERNS

Many empty nesters are part of the sandwich generation. Let's take a look at a few of their stories, to see how they handled the everyday stresses. We'll start with Evelyn:

> *I've told people I am sure I am "middle age" because I feel caught in the middle of helping grown children and helping my parents. One day, however, I realized my daughter might be "middle age" when I became very ill while my husband was in Iraq. She told the doctor she didn't think it was wise for me to live alone anymore. I was age 50! She must have thought I was ancient and I was sure she was going to put me "in the home." My mother says she is no longer middle age and that the worst part about your parents dying is that your name goes to the top of the list.*

Now take a look at what Peggy has to say:

> *I had a brief vacation from being a caretaker of my children for about five years. Then we moved my parents to Texas from Asheville, North Carolina, after thirty years of living 1,000 miles away from each other. We now live three miles apart. I am an only child and my parents still love to tell my friends about the time I was really quiet in my crib on a Sunday afternoon. They assumed I was very tired after a long morning at church but to their surprise, and still delight after fifty years,*

I had used my own human waste to decorate my crib. That story always goes over well with my friends over lunch! I've learned not to take my parents everywhere I go. My life had consisted of bringing babies home from the hospital and carefully working with them to leave the nest, to now being a taxi for my parents as we try to make all their doctor appointments on time. Lunch at Luby's, Quiznos, and Chic-fil-A are now the highlight of our day. Thank goodness my husband loves them even more than I do. With Dad's inability to hear, Mom's inability to remember, and my inability to read anything smaller than an inch, we are quite a threesome.

Don't you love Peggy's positive outlook? You can be just as positive, whether you're caring for a parent or stepping in to help a child. This season won't last forever, Mom. But, instead of fighting it, enjoy the time you have with those you love.

C SMOOTH SAILING

Perhaps you never really heard much about the sandwich generation until now. Maybe you smile as you think about being the "middle" generation, wedged between parents and kids. Think of yourself as the cream in the middle of the cookie. You hold the two pieces together. And you're not alone! You might not be aware of this, but we have a Sandwich Generation Month here in the United States. It takes place during July. The purpose? To bring awareness to (and celebrate the dedication of) those who patiently care for both parents and children.

So, enjoy this season, Mom. If you're blessed to still have your parents, spend as much time as you can with them. Tell them how much you love them. And continue to encourage your grown children, too. They are all looking to you for love and support.

Of course, the best way to get through a situation is to keep the Lord at the center of it. And what better way than by getting His perspective? He's given us plenty of encouragement in His Word to get through the various seasons of our lives. Memorize the following scriptures to bring encouragement and help when you need it.

- *But they that wait upon the LORD shall renew their strength; they shall mount up with wings as eagles; they shall run, and not be weary; and they shall walk, and not faint.*
  ISAIAH 40:31 KJV

- *Yes, even when I am old and gray-headed, O God, forsake me not, [but keep me alive] until I have declared Your mighty strength to [this] generation, and Your might and power to all that are to come.*
  PSALM 71:18 AMP

- *Energize the limp hands, strengthen the rubbery knees. Tell fearful souls, "Courage! Take heart! God is here, right here, on his way to put things right and redress all wrongs. He's on his way! He'll save you!"*
  ISAIAH 35:3–4 MSG

- *Those of us who are strong and able in the faith need to step in and lend a hand to those who falter, and not just do what is most convenient for us. Strength is for service, not status. Each one of us needs to look after the good of the people around us, asking ourselves, "How can I help?"*
  ROMANS 15:1–2 MSG

Chapter 8

A Balancing Act

Helping your eldest to pick a college is one of the greatest educational experiences of life—for the parents. Next to trying to pick his bride, it's the best way to learn that your authority, if not entirely gone, is slipping fast.
SALLY AND JAMES RESTON

BYE-BYE, BIRDIE

Have you ever watched a gymnast during the Olympics doing backflips on the balance beam? (Scary!) You hold your breath, hoping she won't take a tumble. At the end, you breathe a sigh of relief, wondering how in the world she kept from falling. Or maybe you've been to the circus and watched a tightrope walker balance her way from one end of the rope to the other.

Truly, there's only one way to stay balanced—no matter the area of life. Practice makes perfect. That gymnast? She fell hundreds, if not thousands, of times before she finally found her balance. And that tightrope walker? How many times do you imagine she attempted to cross from one side to the other before finally making it the whole way? (Thank goodness for the net below. . .during rehearsals, anyway!)

Practice makes perfect. You've heard it all your life. But never is it truer than now, as you seek to find balance in your life. And it's tough! How do you know how much mothering is too much, for example? Or how to keep a healthy balance in your marriage? How do you know when too much activity is a bad thing? Or when you're wearing your friends out, talking about your married children?

Picture yourself walking on that balance beam. Every time the conversation becomes too one-sided (and who can blame you? You can't help talking about your kids, after all!), you start to tumble. Now imagine yourself on the tightrope. You're doing fine until the phone rings and your son needs a loan to make his car payment. Again. Then, suddenly, you're plunging to the net below.

Take a look at this definition of *balance*: "a stable mental or psychological state; emotional stability."[7] You might say to yourself, "Well, I'm emotionally stable." And perhaps you are. But it might be time to take a step back and ask others who know you well (your spouse, best friend, peers) for their opinion. It could be you're out of balance in an area or two and don't even know it. On the other hand, you might be completely out of balance and know it. . .but wonder how you can ever get the pendulum to swing back toward the middle.

Gillian had a few balance issues during her empty-nest years. For one thing, she had trouble letting go of the "mothering" thing. Whenever her son would call with a problem, she rushed to fix it. When her daughter's marriage was in trouble, she jumped in headfirst (only to regret it later). Gillian's marriage was slightly out of balance, too. She began to lean on her husband, and not just in the usual way. Her phone calls to him were endless, even when he was at work. He finally told her—in a loving way—that she needed to limit herself.

Gillian didn't notice that her friendships were out of balance until her best friend pointed it out. Could she help it if she talked incessantly about her kids and grandkids? And then there was her activity level. After reconciling herself to the empty-nest thing, Gillian went a little crazy, signing up for anything and everything to keep her busy. After a while, she found herself completely exhausted—and completely out of balance where her health was concerned. It seemed that her house of cards would crumble if she didn't make some changes!

---

[7] *The Free Online Dictionary*, s.v. "balance," http://www.thefreedictionary.com/balance">Balance</a> (accessed April 20, 2009).

What about you, Mom? Have you jumped in over your head with activities? Are your mothering skills still causing you to plow forward without thinking things through? Have you lost all sense of balance in your home, redecorating every room and driving your poor husband crazy with carpet and fabric samples? If so, it's time to jump on that balance beam and get to work! Before long, you'll be wobble-free!

> *Adolescence is perhaps nature's way of*
> *preparing parents to welcome the empty nest.*
> KAREN SAVAGE AND PATRICIA ADAMS

SPREADING YOUR WINGS

As you look at your daily life—the things you do in an average day, for instance—can you see any areas that are out of balance? Your eating, perhaps? Your workload? Your marriage? Your finances? Do you spend too much time on some things and not enough on others? Are you starting to feel the strain?

Sometimes it's hard to see from the inside out. You might have to ask a friend for her help. She can point out the areas where you're off-kilter. Thick skin, Mom! You might not be happy with your friend's observations, but she's probably right.

So, let's take a look at the following areas of your life that might be out of balance. Many of these topics have been covered in previous chapters, but hold on to your hat! We're about to look at them from a completely different angle.

- Your marriage
- Your mothering
- Your eating habits
- Your friendships
- Your activities
- Your health
- Your home
- Your checkbook
- Your workload
- Your emotions
- Your boundaries
- Your "ministry" life

Do any of those areas feel a little out of balance in your life right now? If so, don't fret! You've finally got the time to strike a balance. Ask for the Lord's help, and watch what He does!

◯ LIFTOFF!

Okay, Mom. Time to get on the tightrope! Time to bring things into balance. Let's address that list one more time, this time looking for some solutions. It might not be easy, but it's certainly worth the effort, particularly in the long run!

- *Your marriage.* We've mentioned this in prior chapters, but it's worth repeating because this is an area that can—and does—get completely out of balance for some empty nesters. If you're married, the empty-nest years are a great time to get reacquainted with your mate. To discover why you fell in love in the first place. To travel. To start mutual hobbies. To remember all of those things you once wanted to do but didn't have the budget for. However, some empty-nest moms—in an attempt to fill a void left by the children's leaving—begin to inundate their spouses. If you're not careful, your husband might knee-jerk! After all, he's pretty busy right now with his career, if he's like most middle-aged men. Don't become clingy and needy, and don't call him ten or twelve times a day, even if you do need his advice (especially if he's at work). Remember, he can't fill the emptiness. Only God can do that. When you are together, try spicing things up by having candlelight dinners and intimate conversations. Those sweet moments will generally spill over into the bedroom, where the real intimacy occurs.

- *Your mothering.* During the empty-nest years, you might

feel a little hurt (or even offended) by the fact that the kids don't seem to need you anymore. Here's the truth, Mom. They still love you, even if they don't need you. Their current behavior is not a rejection of you as a mom. In fact, if they don't need you, you've done well! The point of being a parent is to become obsolete. Sure, you're still an advisor. You give wise counsel. But here's where things can get out of balance, if you're not careful. Women have a hard time not offering unrequested help. (We have answers for everything, after all!) As a parent, you still want a measure of control (who your child hangs out with, how they spend your money, etc.). But your level of participation in these things depends, at least in part, on whether your child is still "under the umbrella," so to speak. Are you still paying, but have no input in your child's life? Strike a balance. "Our house, our rules. Our money, our rules." If your son or daughter is receiving something from you (car payment, insurance, etc.), you get to have your input. No, that doesn't mean you call your college-age child to remind her to take out the trash, or to tell her what time she needs to be back at her dorm or apartment. But if she's coming and going from your house, it's a different matter. If your child isn't close by, why not set up a plan to e-mail or text, say three or four times a week, if not more? Take a look at Tricia's story:

"When to stop mothering" hit last week and caused a great deal of laughter for all of us. We were supposed to have record cold temps here at home, and even colder in

the city where my grown sons share an apartment. They both have to work out in the elements, and I was really concerned about them, so I sent an e-mail and said, "Just be sure to take precautions and don't do anything foolish." My older son wrote back and said, "I've been doing this for six years now. I have a coat, gloves, a toboggan, and even long underwear. I think I'll be fine." I was laughing by that point, but then he sent me over the edge with a comment about his brother. "I told Jonathan to wear long sleeves and a coat, and not stay out in it too long."

(Isn't it funny how our kids start sounding like parents?)

- *Your eating habits.* The empty-nest years can prove to be tempting when it comes to your food intake. You might swing to the left—eating everything in sight. Or you might swing to the right—dieting to extremes in the hopes of getting your youthful physique back. Neither is recommended. If you struggle in this area, why not set up an appointment with your doctor or a nutritionist? They can help you find the proper nutritional balance. Nibbling on sweets is okay in moderation, but you might be eating to fill a void. Dieting in moderation is fine, too, but if you're starving yourself you've thrown things out of whack. Take a look at Pamela's story:

    When my daughter—an only child—abruptly moved out of state to start a new job, I reacted by overeating. Might sound weird, but food was comforting to me.

*Whenever I got really lonely, I would eat something.
Because I lived alone, no one really saw how much I was
eating (or what I was eating, for that matter). I was
on my own. Before long, I'd put on thirty pounds. My
daughter came back for a visit, and I could see the shock
in her expression. After she left, I did an about-face,
but probably went a little overboard. I tossed all of the
junk food (always a good idea), then began a stringent
diet and exercise program. The thirty pounds came off,
along with ten more. While this might have been a
good thing, even the diet was out-of-balance. I talked
incessantly about vitamins and supplements. I couldn't
have a meal without discussing the calorie count with
all in attendance. Unfortunately, my friends didn't want
to play along. After a while, I think I drove them all a
little crazy. I finally had to back down, realizing that
preaching to them wasn't the way to convert them to my
way of thinking. I eventually realized that I'd been going
overboard, because of my own self-focus. Unfortunately,
in all my zeal, I lost too much weight too quickly and
several pounds eventually worked their way back on.
I've since joined a Christian weight-loss group and have
learned that I'm an emotional eater. I have to watch
myself very closely because I tend to operate in "extremes."
These days, I'm trying to strike a balance!*

- *Your friendships.* Perhaps it never occurred to you that
  your friendships could be knocked out of balance. . .but
  they can. We can spend far too much time talking about

our kids in front of our friends (to the point where they become disinterested). If there are long silences at the table or if there are rolled eyes when you're talking about your kids, there might be a problem. The empty-nest season is the perfect time to broaden your horizons. Watch the news so you can talk about what's going on outside your box. Instead of sitting around commiserating about your kids with your friends, go to the theater. Take up a mutual hobby. And when you are seated around the lunch table with girlfriends, the greatest way to strike a balance is to find the quietest person at the table and ask, "So how are things going with you?" In other words, turn your focus. Don't be a needy friend (unless you're truly in need, and even then you should probably seek help from a counselor, as well as a trusted friend). And if you're struggling with a friend who's too needy (perhaps another empty nester), it might be time to take a step back. All things in balance, Mom! This is what Jean had to say:

I've always had a great group of girlfriends, and we all went through empty nest together. After a while, though, we noticed that our conversations were always about the kids. We decided we needed a change, so we put together a plan of action. Now, once a year, we all take a trip together. We go to a bed-and-breakfast, usually. Often in some small town no one's heard of. In short, we get away from things. . .together. That gives us a lot more to talk about! We now spend much of our "together" time talking about last year's trip or planning for next year's!

- *Your activities.* If you're like most empty-nest moms, you like to stay busy. Maybe you overload your day. Work. The gym. Dinner with your hubby. Art class on Monday night. Bible study on Tuesday night. On and on the list goes. While it's good to stay busy, you'll eventually burn out if you're not careful. Consider Rhonda's story:

> When my kids left home, I had the perfect antidote for what ailed me. Stay busy, busy, busy. I dove in. Took over the leadership of our local book club. Joined a gym. Volunteered to work in the children's ministry. Tried my hand at jewelry making. Took a class at the community college. You name it, I tried it. At the end of it all, I was absolutely exhausted but didn't really feel those things filled the empty spot inside. I finally prayed about it all and lightened my load. I still go to my Bible study and the gym (though not as often as before). During my "down" time, I try to take better care of myself (eating right, getting a massage occasionally, and enjoying a pedicure with a friend). I've decided many of those other things were just "fillers." Now I'm asking the Lord to fill me up, instead!

- *Your health.* The middle years are the perfect time to refocus on your health. Supplements. Doctor visits. Mammograms. Pap smears. It's a good idea to stay on top of these things. A lot of middle-aged women struggle with very real physical problems: arthritis, blood sugar issues, blood pressure, headaches, etc. And then there are the biggies—breast cancer, ovarian cancer, heart disease, and so on. If there was ever a time to strike a balance with your health, it's now! Perhaps you're overdue for a physical. Or maybe you haven't been feeling well but have been scared to express it to anyone other than yourself. Why not bite the bullet and call your doctor today? In order for you to pour into the lives of others (your aging parents, your spouse, your grown children, your grandchildren), you've got to be in the best possible shape.

- *Your home.* If you're a Suzy Homemaker, then the empty-nest years are going to be a blast! You'll have so much fun redecorating, hanging new curtains and wallpaper, rearranging furniture, and so forth. However, if you're not careful, you might very well drive your husband crazy and wreak havoc on your budget! Take Leslie, for example:

> *Okay, I have to confess. . .when the kids left, I wasn't one of those who was sad to see them go. On the contrary! I'd been waiting for years to get my house to myself. My husband wanted a game room (a media/pool table area) and I wanted an honest-to-goodness craft room. (For years I'd been making do with my kitchen table.) On top of all that, the living room needed an overhaul and the kitchen was crying out for new cabinets and countertops. So, the minute our youngest headed off to college, I flew into action. Within months, the whole house was changed. You'd think that would be enough, but no. I went a little overboard. I didn't like some of the changes I'd made, so I*

changed them again. And again. Before long, it was like a game of musical chairs. People would come to my house and say things like, "Hey, wasn't that wall blue the last time I was here?" I would just sigh. My husband finally put a stop to it all. And I finally realized what I'd been doing all along. I was somehow trying to erase some of the memories of my child-rearing days, because facing them was just too painful. (Turned out, I did miss those kids after all!)

- *Your checkbook.* You've probably heard the old saying, "Money makes the world go around." Well, it's true. . .at least in part! Empty nesters have a lot of financial issues to deal with: college tuition, room and board, weddings, children with legitimate needs, grandchildren who need to be spoiled, etc. This can be a very trying time on the pocketbook. It's also a time you really need to keep things in balance. You want to do the right thing, but you don't want to go overboard. Take a look at Debbie's story:

My husband and I faced an interesting situation when our daughter—a single mother—got behind on her mortgage. With the downturn in the economy, she'd been forced to take a pay cut at work. She came to us, asking for a loan to get caught up. We could tell it totally humiliated her to do so. My husband and I prayed about it and loaned her the money. Then, about three months later, our daughter was in the same jam all over again. This time we wrestled with what to do. If we got in the habit of always giving, would she come to depend on us? Thankfully, she picked up some extra hours at work and was able to make the mortgage payment, albeit late. She still struggles, but we take each challenge as it comes. My husband and I have a new motto: We don't offer assistance, even when asked, unless we pray about it and feel a release from the Lord to do so.

- *Your workload.* Many middle-aged women throw themselves into their work, to the point of exhaustion. Perhaps you've spent many years waiting for the time when you can finally further your own career. With no children needing you to come home early, you may be tempted to take on extra hours at your place of employment. As with anything else, however, the Bible urges moderation. Also, look to the reason you're loading your plate. Are you filling your day with good things that benefit or are you merely filling your day? And what of your spouse, if you have one? Have you chosen work over marriage? Be careful here as the enemy would love to derail you from the track the Lord has set you on. Add things to your schedule with care and be ready to eliminate anything that gets between you and God!

- *Your emotions.* Often our homes empty at about the same time our bodies are going through what our mothers called "the change." Menopause. Indeed this is a four-letter word to some, as the coming of this season can also mean a flurry of new and not-so-welcome emotions for some.

Even if you've not yet reached that time in your life, an empty nest can mean a mama bird whose feathers can get ruffled more than before. Recognize this is normal and know that this, too, shall pass. Talk to your spouse about your feelings and, if necessary, your doctor as well. Take a look at Pat's story:

I didn't handle pre-menopause very well. My emotions were completely out of whack. And now that I'm facing the real deal—the dreaded "M" word—I'm struggling even more. Hot flashes? I have enough to heat an entire house! Emotional outbursts? I can't seem to help myself. Add to that other puzzling symptoms—joint pain, heart flutterings, and so on—and you can see that I'm a wreck. Some of the time, anyway. I've never been a crier, but these past few months, I've shed plenty of tears. Why? I can rarely put my finger on any one thing. I'm just emotional across-the-board. My doctor and I recently discussed my options and we chose to go the natural route. I'm praying it works! In the meantime, pray for my husband and kids! Sometimes I blubber all over them. . . but don't know why!

Can you relate to Pat? Have you been through the very real "shift" in life (menopause)? If so, then your emotions can be ragged, fragile things. Truly your best plan of action (along with visiting your doctor) is to give those emotions to the Lord. He created them, you know!

- *Your boundaries.* We all need boundaries in our lives. They're there for our protection. . .our good. They help us keep things in balance. This is definitely true of the empty-nest mom. You must decide where your boundaries are at the earliest possible moment. Once tested, these boundaries can bring comfort or trouble, depending on who is ignoring them. Overstepping boundaries can damage the relationship between you and your grown children. Take a look at Norah's story to see how she handled this very delicate issue:

> *I have to confess, I was always a little worried about how I would be perceived as a mother-in-law. I think I babied my son too much and wondered how his new wife would take that. With an empty house (and no one to really "help") I started encouraging my daughter-in-law with her cooking and housekeeping skills. Well, I thought I was encouraging, anyway. Turns out, I was hurting her feelings. My mothering skills went a little bit too far, I guess, though I never realized it until my son brought it up. I never thought about the fact that she might perceive my comments as offensive, but apparently she did. I've since apologized. . .and backed off. It's hard, because I still have the desire to "mother" inside of me. I guess I was just looking for a new "kid" as a candidate and my daughter-in-law fit the bill.*

- *Your "ministry" life.* If you haven't learned to put the brakes on your ministries or volunteer work, where do you start?

You're like a kid with a driver's license for the first time. Where do you stop? Never considered the answer to that question? Well, consider this: You may not know where the stopping point is until you've passed it. Pay careful attention to prayer as you add each item to an ever-increasing schedule of duties and responsibilities.

> *When you are busy being a wife and mother*
> *that's the testing and proving ground.*
> *When they are all gone it's time to assimilate*
> *what you've learned, gain wisdom from it all,*
> *and share your wisdom with others who are in*
> *the testing and proving ground.*
>
> CHERRI TAYLOR

◖ FLIGHT PATTERNS

Different strokes for different folks. Right, Mom? Maybe you're able to balance one way and your best friend, another. That's okay. God is able to use different people and different circumstances to bring about different results for different people. (Whew! That was a mouthful!)

Let's take a look at a couple of stories to see how some moms kept things in balance during their empty-nest years. The first is from Cecelia:

> *After reconciliation with my children, God replaced those lost times with more than we could have hoped or prayed for. My daughter passed away last year and my son is now married to the most wonderful young lady. My way of mothering is much prayer. I call them whenever the mood strikes or I feel the nudge of the Spirit to do so. I only give advice if they ask for it. My daughter-in-law asked me recently if I would take care of a situation with my son and I politely told her the best way I could, "Honey, he's your problem now!"*

If you have married children, you can certainly relate to that last line! Now let's look at a story from Sandra:

> *Now that we're empty nesters, our relationship with both sons has steadied. All during the teen and young adult years, it seems like we were just one big pendulum, swinging from one extreme (needy, immature,*

> *tantrums, irresponsibility, etc.) to another (distant, no*
> *communication, etc.). Now, with them both on their*
> *own, they call and talk to us, share their lives with us. We*
> *are friends—even on Facebook! It's very beautiful.*

Isn't that a cool story? Becoming friends with your grown children is the ultimate goal. Sure, they will still look to you as a parent, but even that will change as they age. You still deserve the respect, but the friendship of your children sweetens the pot even further! All of this is possible if you live a balanced, healthy life. (Your kids will learn from your example!)

Regardless of how God chooses to move during this wobbly season, allow Him the opportunity to do what He needs to do to bring things in your life into balance. Your health—and your children—will thank you!

◠ SMOOTH SAILING

So, how do you think you're doing keeping things in balance, Mom? Ready to jump on that balance beam or take a waltz across the tightrope on your tiptoes? Just remember that the only true way to balance anything is with Jesus Christ at the center. Put Him in His rightful place and you'll do just fine!

- *Overwork makes for restless sleep. Overtalk shows you up as a fool.*
  ECCLESIASTES 5:3 MSG

- *Though the army besiege me, my heart will not fear; though war break out against me, even then will I be confident.*
  PSALM 27:3 NIV

- *You should clothe yourselves instead with the beauty that comes from within, the unfading beauty of a gentle and quiet spirit, which is so precious to God.*
  1 PETER 3:4 NLT

- *Better is a handful with quietness than both hands full with painful effort, a vain striving after the wind and a feeding on it.*
  ECCLESIASTES 4:6 AMP

  Never lend your car to anyone to whom you have given birth.
  ERMA BOMBECK

Chapter 9

BUILDING YOUR NEST IN HIS COURTS

Having babies is fun, but babies grow up into people.
M*A*S*H, COLONEL POTTER

◐ BYE-BYE, BIRDIE

Let's talk about that mama bird one more time. . .only, this time let's go all the way back to the day those baby chicks erupted from their little shells. What joy she must've felt as they poked their little heads through to the outside world.

You are now that baby bird, Mom! You're poking your head through to an unfamiliar world, wondering if you will make it. Here's the good news. . .you will! You are being reborn, in a sense. Coming alive. Figuring out who you are! Can you sense the excitement as you think about the possibilities? ("Free at last!")

Let's go back to a subject we touched on briefly in an earlier chapter. Remember that swallow who built her nest in the temple courts? The one who stayed close to the Lord? You are that little swallow, Mom. Beyond anything we've addressed in the pages of this book, you've got to know who you are in Christ. . .and you've got to stay close to Him. Learn to be "at home" with the God of the universe, and any problem—empty nest or otherwise—is manageable. Build your nest in His sanctuary. It's not too late, even if the little birdies have flown the coop.

Many of the women in the Bible learned this lesson. They drew near to God and He drew near to them. (Why not pause for a moment and think about some of the biblical greats who learned this lesson. . .Eve, Hannah, Naomi, and Mary, the mother of Jesus, to name a few. Oh, how much they can teach us!)

Gillian learned, too, though it took a little time. She tried so many things, made so many mistakes before finally coming to grips with the fact that God was her supplier. He met her needs—emotionally, psychologically, spiritually, and physically—when she finally came clean and told Him about her struggles.

Now it's your turn, Mama Bird. Perhaps you've got some lingering issues that you haven't dealt with. Maybe you're still lonely, even after reading the stories in this book. Or maybe you're going through a rough time with one of your children. Perhaps you've tragically lost a son or daughter in a way you never anticipated. Or maybe you're going through a rough season with one of your parents. No matter what you're facing, the God of the universe longs for you to build your nest near Him so that He can bring healing and wholeness.

The journey in and through the empty-nest years is one you will remember for the rest of your life. How you react to the transitions in your life is completely up to you. . .no one else. That's why you've got to stay close to the Lord, even when things get hard. With His help, you can and will thrive during this very volatile season!

> *Sweet bird! thy bow'r is ever green,*
> *Thy sky is ever clear;*
> *Thou has't no sorrow in thy song,*
> *No winter in thy year.*
> JOHN LOGAN

SPREADING YOUR WINGS

We've covered a lot of issues in this book—everything from menopause to parenting our parents to rescuing our kids. The following list is a little different. We're going to close out by talking about some specific empty nesters who face the biggest obstacles. Perhaps you fall into this category. Even if you don't, please take the time to read through this information, so that you can help others who might be facing these issues.

Empty nesters who have it exceptionally tough:

- The grieving mom (one who has lost a child to death or dire circumstances)

- The divorced mom (one who has no husband to support her)

- The disappointed mom (one who is sad at the way her children turned out, or in some way disappointed in herself as a mother)

- The menopausal mom (one who can't seem to control the changes she's going through)

- The stepparent or adoptive mom (one who is facing all sorts of unique issues)

- The angry mom (one who is, perhaps, still carrying unforgiveness and/or pain)

What do you think? Can you relate to any items on that list? Perhaps you may even fit into more than one category. If so, hang on for the ride! If not, take a look at some suggestions and ideas that might help out a friend in need.

◐ LIFTOFF!

Before we get too deep into this teaching, let's address one very simple thing: the word *empty*. It's such a negative word, isn't it? Perhaps "empty" nest isn't the most encouraging way to label your situation. Perhaps you should call this season "liftoff," as this section implies. You are, after all, taking a flight of your own. And even though it may be difficult at times, it's one where you will eventually learn to soar.

Let's pause to offer a few suggestions to those who are genuinely struggling.

- *The grieving mom.* Oh, how God grieves with those who grieve! If you're facing empty nest because of the death of a child, the presence of the Lord is truly the only way you will make it through. May your heavenly Father wrap you in His arms and give you the strength you need to face each new day. Let's take a look at Gail's story:

    I was only forty-two when my only child—my daughter, Lori—was killed in a car accident. The whole thing was (and is) like a dream. A nightmare, really. She was on her way back to college when she lost control of the car. Mercifully, she died right away. I was told she didn't suffer. At least I can be grateful for that. The weeks following were a total haze. They were filled with loving friends and family members, all trying to say and do the right things. But I was inconsolable. It's now been seven years and I'm slowly healing. It took two of those seven years before I would even touch her room. I left everything exactly as it was. My husband and I have since turned the room into an office, though we've set up a special area with her teddy bears, prom dress, etc. It's still hard to think of ourselves as "empty nesters". It is truly only through our relationship with the Lord that my husband and I have made it through. Well, that, and the continual outpouring of love from our friends. Though I couldn't receive their words the first couple of years, they are finally sinking in now. There's something so comforting about a person who takes the time to wrap me in her arms and tell me that she loves me. One of the biggest lessons I've learned from Lori's death is that nothing really belongs to me. It all belongs to God. I am so thankful to have been a mom and to have experienced how to care for someone else. Everything on this earth is on loan and temporary. Daily decisions and opportunities come and go. It has challenged me to be a good steward of my time. I will continue to enjoy my transformational journey into the likeness of His Son.

If you've lost a child—or if you have a child who's run away from home or left under bitter circumstances—then you can surely relate to Gail's story. If you're in this position, please take the time to read the final section of this chapter. It will help you release that pain to a loving God, who stands with arms extended.

- *The divorced mom.* If you've been through the heartache of divorce, then you are already well acquainted with grief and loss. In so many ways, your "family unit" can seem to be unraveling before your very eyes. And then, when it's time for the kids to leave, you're left to face things without someone standing next to you. Clearly, the only way to get through this transition is with the help of the Lord. He will be a Husband to you and a Father to your children. He adores you! You are His bride! So, whenever you feel those familiar pangs. . .whenever you wish you had someone else to share your feelings with, remember. . . you do. He's standing with arms outstretched. Take a look at Sarah's story. If you've been through a divorce, chances are, you can relate:

> *Within a three-year period, I lost my husband (due to divorce), my father (he died after a bout with multiple myeloma), and my sister (who died in her sleep at the age of forty-five). In the middle of all of this, my youngest daughter got married. I found myself completely alone in the house. About a month after the wedding, I was in an accident that left me in a wheelchair for about a month. During that time, I fell into the deepest pit imaginable. I felt completely lost and alone. Thankfully, my friends swept in around me. So did my grown children. They nurtured and cared for me and helped me get back on my*

feet again (literally!). It was quite a valley, but I have to admit, the Lord met me there. All of my tears, all of my heartache. . .it all came out at once. (I'd bottled things up inside—pain from the divorce, pain from losing my loved ones, and pain from my children leaving the nest.) I came out of that valley into the sunlight once again. My kids are truly my heroes. They've walked with me every step of the way. And the Lord has allowed the grieving to "grow" me into the woman I am today: stronger, healthier, and ready to face tomorrow head-on.

- *The disappointed mom.* Are you one of those moms who is disappointed in the way her children turned out or, perhaps, disappointed in herself? Maybe your parenting skills weren't the best. Maybe you didn't come to know the Lord until your children were grown. God still hasn't given up on them, and neither should you. If you're facing the heartache of a child who is away from the Lord, stand strong! Don't give up. "The effectual fervent prayer of a righteous man [or woman!] availeth much" (James 5:16 KJV). The enemy of your soul would love nothing more than to see you give in to the fear that your child will never change. Keep the faith, Mom. As you read Peg's story, see if it doesn't encourage you.

My kids weren't raised in church. There's a simple reason for that. I didn't go to church. I didn't come to know the Lord until I was in my forties. By then, my kids were mostly grown. They were off doing their own thing

*and not interested in Mom's "spiritual experience." I tried
to reach out to them with the gospel message but didn't
do a very good job of it. Both of my boys entered the work
world and did very well financially. But I knew there
was a gaping hole in their hearts, in part from the loss
of their father (my husband left when they were small)
and because everyone has a God-shaped vacuum inside. I
prayed for years. Twenty years, to be precise. And the way
the Lord won my boys was, indeed, a miracle. I remarried
a few years ago—to a wonderful, godly man. He stepped
in and became the father my boys never had. Through
his gentle, encouraging love, the boys eventually came to
know the Lord.*

- *The menopausal mom.* All women go through menopause,
but not all have the same symptoms. Some sail through
with little problem. Others find that "season" the most
difficult of their lives (particularly those who go through
early menopause and/or those who had hoped to have
more children). If you're going through menopause at
the same time your nest is emptying out, emotions can
run pretty high. Help is available, Mom. There are so
many options for menopausal women today, but it's
more important than ever to talk to your doctor before
beginning a regimen, even a natural one. Only your
doctor can do the necessary blood work to determine your
hormone levels. Take a look at Lottie's story:

My husband and I had two precious children in the

early years of our marriage, but when the youngest was in
junior high, we decided we wanted to try for one more.
Sadly, I was never able to get pregnant. (This was before
the days of infertility testing, by the way.) When I was
thirty-nine, my period stopped. Stopped. I was so shocked.
I wasn't ready to be done with that phase of my life yet.
I did a lot of begging—with God, I mean. I wanted
another child. Unfortunately, that never happened. Early
onset menopause took care of that, once and for all. The
Lord has a sense of humor, though. My husband and
I ended up going on several missions trips to Romania
when we were in our late forties (after our kids were out
of the house). We met two beautiful little girls and ended
up adopting them. Now our nest is very full once more!

What do you think of that, Mom? Can you imagine starting
over after menopause? For some, this is the perfect solution!

- *The stepparent or adoptive mom.* This is a tricky one. These
  folks face all sorts of out-of-the-box issues. If you're a
  stepparent and your stepchild has left your home under
  not-so-great circumstances, you are sure to face feelings of
  rejection, along with empty-nest feelings. And if you're an
  adoptive parent whose grown child is getting to know his
  or her birth mother, it's likely you're facing issues unique
  to you. Here's the good news, Mom. God hasn't fallen
  off His throne. He was there when that child came into
  your life, and He's still there, walking you through this
  season. And it is a season, you know. Your nest might be

empty now, but it's likely your kiddos—adopted, step, or otherwise—will fly back home. Take a look at Helen's story:

> *My husband and I adopted our daughter when she was three. She had vague memories of her birth mother, most of them not good. Imagine our surprise when, at age eighteen, our daughter announced she wanted to meet her again. We were floored. However, I also knew—hard as this was—that it would be worse to intervene or to try to stop her. We located her birth mother in a short period of time and before long, the two were inseparable. My heart felt like it would break when my daughter—now nineteen—announced that she wanted to live with her birth mother. Again, I knew better than to stop her. This was something she needed to do to feel whole and complete. Now, six years later, we are all friends. My daughter is married and has a baby girl. We're all involved in the baby's life. We're truly one big happy family.*

- *The angry mom.* Some women react to the empty nest with anger. Maybe they're angry at an ex-husband who didn't help raise the children, who didn't provide adequately. Maybe they're mad at the child, who put the family through untold grief during his or her teen years. Maybe they're angry with themselves, for not doing a better job. Anger itself isn't a sin. Acting on it is. If you're dealing with feelings of anger, then it's likely you're carrying unforgiveness. There's no better time than now to let go of that. Forgive. . .that you might be forgiven (Mark 11:25). Let it go. Then watch as the Lord washes away your angst. (Only He can do it, you know.) Take a look at Liz's story to see how she handled this situation:

My story isn't terribly dramatic, but maybe some will find it helpful. My husband and I raised our kids (a boy and a girl) in church. We were a fairly "normal" Christian family in most respects (had the usual amount of "stuff" during the teenage years, but nothing drastic). I did pretty well when my son went off to college, but then my daughter (a year and a half younger) fell in love with an older guy that we didn't care for and decided to marry him. Quickly. Two months later they were married. My house was empty. I was really angry—with her, for making what I thought was a foolish decision. With my son-in-law, for enticing her to marry him. And with God, who allowed it all to happen. For a while, I let that anger drive me. I wasn't terribly polite to my son-in-law and I even let a wall go up between my daughter and myself. Then the Lord began to do business with me. He forced me to look at my unforgiveness. Not easy or pleasant. In the end, I had to let go of all bitterness and forgive. I am happy to say that my relationship with my daughter has never been stronger and I now love that son-in-law like my own son! They are going to have a baby in a couple of months, and I can't wait to be a grandmother for the first time!

How does that story make you feel, Mom? Have you ever been angry with a grown child, or perhaps a son- or daughter-in-law? It's time to let it go. Give it to the Lord. As you forgive. . .He forgives. Only then, can you walk in wholeness.

As women, we walk through many different seasons, many different difficulties. But God is there, ready to guide us, every step of the way. Draw near to Him. . .and He will draw near to you (James 4:8)!

C ENTERING HIS COURTS

We're going to close out the book by taking a little detour. . .into the Holy of Holies. Perhaps you're still struggling with some issues we haven't discussed in this book. Maybe your feelings are deep, and your anguish is deeper still. Maybe you're suffering through the loss of a child or a divorce and haven't found your bearings. Or maybe you're just feeling a little lost since your youngest went away to college. You're confused about who you are and where you fit in. Truly, the only place you will ever find the guidance you need is in the Lord's presence.

Before we do that, however, it's important to note one thing: the enemy of your soul doesn't want you to "go deep" with God. He always wants to pull your nest away from the courts of the King because he knows what will happen once you draw near. When you stick close to the Lord, you can't help but discover that God has a plan for you in this next stage of your life! But never fear! As soon as you enter that secret, holy place with your heavenly Father, the enemy slithers away in the grass, knowing he's met more than his match.

If you've never done a study of the Holy of Holies, this would be a great time to do so. In Old Testament times, the people of God had to rely on animal sacrifice as atonement for their sin. Once a year, the high priest would go into a tiny room called the Holy of Holies (or Most Holy Place) to represent the people and to lay their sins on the altar before God. This small room was an inner sanctuary of the tabernacle. Only the man of God was welcome inside.

The Holy of Holies was a "set-apart" place and in many respects, a fearful place, for the priest symbolically carried in the sins, anguishes, and pains of the people.

Think about that high priest for a moment. Can you hear his heart thumping as he pushes back the veil and enters that inner sanctum? Can you see his hands shaking as he burns the incense and sprinkles sacrificial animal blood? Can you sense the relief as the ritual comes to its completion? Must've been pretty heavy stuff—to come in with so many sins on your hands.

If you're a blood-bought believer of Jesus Christ, you recognize that His work on the cross was the final payment for our sins. He paid it all on Calvary. And (what an awesome story this is!) just after He died, the veil in the temple was torn in two. No longer do you have to be a high priest to enter the Holy of Holies. God desires that all of us—scarred, exhausted, sinful, tainted people—enter. Why? Not to atone for our sins. No, Jesus took care of that part for us. We are now invited into the Holy of Holies for personal, intimate time with the Lord of the universe. The only sacrifice He wants from us is a sacrifice of praise. . .a bending of our knee and our will.

Picture yourself walking into the throne room of God, His Most Holy Place. Imagine coming with your heart in your hands and laying it on the altar so that He can do His perfect work. Can you hear yourself calling out the names of your children, asking the Lord to draw them to Himself? Consider the condition of your heart as you openly expose your deepest wounds, your most painful experiences. Give Him whatever you're dealing with—menopause symptoms, fears over your aging parents, the spiritual condition of your children, your marriage, any feelings of loneliness. Then watch in awe as your Savior takes your heart in His gentle hands, reshapes and remolds it, then breathes new life over your situation, offering healing, hope, and grace.

We don't have to be afraid of God. That's it, in a nutshell. There's no reason to fear getting real with Him. You can bare your soul, and you won't be rejected. You can share your angst, your pain, your deepest longings, your hopeful desires, your wants and wishes, and He will sweep you into His arms.

What are you bringing to Him today, Mom? A child who isn't walking with the Lord? Feelings of loss? A list of things you would like to accomplish during this phase of your life? The desire to see your marriage and your friendships grow stronger? A new job? The admission that you need Him now more than ever? Whatever you hold in your hands, place it on the altar, then watch the Lord take it and shape it into something of great beauty.

⟲ FINAL THOUGHTS

Remember these words from the beginning of the book?: "Becoming an empty nester is tricky. It's an awesome, amazing, freeing, terrible, horrible, no-good, very bad time. . .filled with ups and downs, ins and outs. You're struggling to balance those delicious feelings of freedom with the grief of watching your children make their way into the world. . .without you! Talk about a conundrum!" Well, those words still apply. You've come a long way, baby, but there's still a ways to go. You're on a learning curve and need to "grace" yourself as much as possible.

During this season, be careful not to spend too much time analyzing whether you did or didn't do a good job in the past. Consider the words of Paul to the church at Philippi: "Brethren, I do not count myself to have apprehended; but one thing I do, forgetting those things which are behind and reaching forward to those things which are ahead, I press toward the goal for the prize of the upward call of God in Christ Jesus" (Philippians 3:13–14 NKJV).

Looking back is dangerous. Chances are, you did a fine job, anyway. Maybe even better than expected, if your circumstances were trying. If you made mistakes—*and who among us didn't?*—you still have time to watch God move in the days and years ahead. You are, after all, pressing toward the goal for the prize!

One final thought. . . You might think your teaching years are behind you, but they are not. Just wait till those calls start coming in: "Mom, the baby is crying and I don't know how to make her stop!" Yep. The teaching (and the learning) goes on forever. Now that your children are adults (your peers—gasp!)

you can teach them more profound things because their mindset is different. So is yours. It's a level playing field now.

Never fear, Mom. They're still watching you and learning by example. They will learn from you as you embrace new things, as you develop new skills, as you grow closer to the Lord.

So, peer over the edge of that nest, Mama Bird! The skies ahead are bright and sunny. C'mon, spread those wings. It's time to take flight!

> *The reason birds can fly and we can't is simply that they have perfect faith, for to have faith is to have wings.*
> JAMES MATTHEW BARRIE

About the Authors

Janice Hanna, who also writes under the name Janice Thompson, is the author of over fifty novels and nonfiction books for the Christian market. She makes her home in the Houston area near two of her four grown daughters. Between 2004 and 2008 all four of her daughters got married. She went from being the "Kool-Aid mom" to having a very empty nest in a short period of time. Though it took some adjustment, she has since grown to love her new life. Most days, Janice can be found playing with her grandbabies, directing musical comedies for the stage, or writing and editing with her two miniature dachshunds at her side. Ah, the life!

Kathleen Y'Barbo is a tenth-generation Texan and a mother of three grown sons and a teenage daughter. She is a graduate of Texas A&M University and an award-winning novelist of over forty Christian novels and novellas. Her first published work jumped onto the Christian Booksellers Association bestseller list in its first month of release. Kathleen is a former treasurer for the American Christian Fiction Writers, and is a member of the Author's Guild, Inspirational Writers Alive, Words for the Journey Christian Writers Guild, and the Fellowship of Christian Authors. In addition, she is a sought-after speaker, and her four grown children think she's a pretty cool mom, too. . . most of the time, anyway.

RESOURCES

WEB SITES:

- *Psychology Today*: Empty Nest Syndrome: http://www.psychologytoday.com/conditions/emptynest.html

- Christian Books for Women: Empty-Nest Syndrome: http://www.christian-books-for-women.com/empty-nest-syndrome.html

- Empty Nest Support Services: www.emptynestsupport.com

- WebMD: Menopause: http://www.webmd.com/menopause/

- Hot Flashes from Heaven, Ronna Snyder: http://www.ronnasnyder.com/

- Seasoned Sisters: Practical tips for making life *Fantastic After 40!* http://www.seasonedsisters.com/

- Sandwich Generation: The Cluttered Nest Syndrome: http://marriage.about.com/cs/sandwich/a/sandwichgen.htm

- The Sandwich Generation: http://www.thesandwichgeneration.com/

- Boomer Babes: http://www.boomerbabesrock.com/

- Pamela D. Blair, PhD: http://www.pamblair.com/

- Boomer Women Speak: http://www.boomerwomenspeak.com/

- National Association for Baby Boomer Women: http://www.boomerwomenspeak.com/

- The Daily Bible Booster at Peggie's Place: http://www.peggiesplace.com/booster116.htm

- Author Grace Fox: http://www.gracefox.com/

- Author Janice (Hanna) Thompson: www.janiceathompson.com

- Author Kathleen Y'Barbo: www.kathleenybarbo.com

FOR FURTHER READING

- *Barbara & Susan's Guide to the Empty Nest: Discovering New Purpose, Passion, & Your Next Great Adventure* (Family Life Publishing) by Barbara Rainey and Susan Yates

- *Beyond the Mommy Years: How to Live Happily Ever After. . .After the Kids Leave Home* (Springboard Press) by Carin Rubenstein

- *Boundaries with Kids* (Zondervan) by Henry Cloud and John Townsend

- *Chicken Soup for the Soul: Empty Nesters: 101 Stories about Surviving and Thriving When the Kids Leave Home* (Chicken Soup for the Soul) by Jack Canfield, Mark Victor Hansen, Carol McAdoo Rehme, and Patricia Cena Evans

- *Fantastic After 40!: The Savvy Woman's Guide to Her Best Season of Life* (Harvest House) by Pam Farrel

- *Feathers from My Nest: A Mother's Reflections* (B&H Books) by Beth Moore

- *Hot Flashes from Heaven: Help When Midlife and Menopause Meet* (Harvest House) by Ronna Snyder

- *Second Calling: Finding Passion and Purpose for the Rest of Your Life* (Thomas Nelson) by Dale Hanson Bourke

- *Second Half of Marriage, The* (Zondervan) by David and Claudia Arp

- *Setting Boundaries with Your Adult Children: Six Steps to Hope and Healing for Struggling Parents* (Harvest House) by Allison Bottke

- *10 Great Dates for Empty Nesters* (Zondervan) by David and Claudia Arp

- *When You're Facing the Empty Nest: Avoiding Midlife Meltdown When Your Child Leaves Home* (Bethany House) by Mary Ann Froehlich

- *You Know You're an Empty Nester When. . . .A Hilarious Look at Life After Kids* (S.P.I. Books) by Dianne Sundby, PhD, and Jeff Law

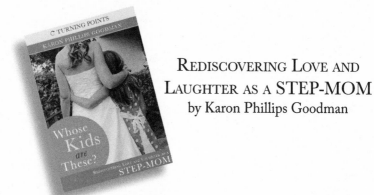